BROTHER CROW,
SISTER CORN

BROTHER CROW, SISTER CORN

TRADITIONAL AMERICAN INDIAN GARDENING

CAROL BUCHANAN

TEN SPEED PRESS
BERKELEY, CALIFORNIA

Ten Speed Press
Post Office Box 7123
Berkeley, California 94707

Distributed in Australia by E. J. Dwyer Pty. Ltd., in Canada by Publishers Group West, in New Zealand by Tandem Press, in South Africa by Real Books, in Singapore and Malaysia by Berkeley Books, and in the United Kingdom and Europe by Airlift Books.

Design by Toni Tajima
Cover photograph by Scott Vlaun

Library of Congress Cataloging-in-Publication Data:
  Buchanan, Carol, 1952–
  Brother Crow, Sister Corn / Carol Buchanan
      p.   cm.
    Includes bibliographical references and index.
    ISBN 0-89815-850-8
      1. Indians of North America—Agriculture. I. Title.
  E98.A3B83   1997
  306.3'64'08997—dc20   96–32204
                                                                              CIP

First printing 1997
Printed in Canada
1 2 3 4 5 — 01 00 99 98 97

To Charlotte O. French and
in memory of William B. French

CONTENTS

FOREWORD

"For many gardening people, the connection between cultivated vegetables, particularly corn, and themselves is so close as to be flesh of flesh. Human life is bought with sacrifice and sealed with the life of the corn plant, as it is with the lives of the deer, bison, or salmon."

BROTHER CROW, SISTER CORN is a poetically written and well-researched book that chronicles American Indian gardening from pre-European contact to modern times. With this important work Carol Buchanan has made a threefold contribution to the art and science of American gardening. First, she has offered a fresh perspective on our collective gardening history. Second, she has provided, through her discussions of tribal gardening practices, some wonderful examples of useful gardening adaptations to adverse climatic conditions. Finally, with respect and clarity, she has given greater exposure to American Indian cultures, their gardening sophistication, and their spiritual relationship with the natural world.

As an avid gardener of American Indian heritage (Ojibwa) and professor of landscape architecture I have always been interested in the contribution of Native peoples to the art and science of gardening. To my knowledge, *Brother Crow, Sister Corn* is the first book to address this subject in a meaningful way. It has documented the gardening world of American Indians, from creation stories to trade networks. I am truly impressed with the breadth and depth of the research undertaken to tell the story of so many native cultures' gardening practices.

The descriptions of ceremonial life and spirituality that grew out of these gardening traditions are a fascinating part of this book. I am not familiar with another source that as clearly and comprehensively communicates the spiritual beliefs of so many Indian peoples. *Brother Crow, Sister Corn* should be a touchstone for anyone who is interested in the spiritual dimensions of gardening. It has brought greater spiritual depth to my own relationship with the natural world.

From a practical point of view, this book is a wonderful reference for gardening. After a summer of drought and endless sun, an experiment with Zuni waffle gardening is scheduled for the spring, and I will approach companion planting with new vigor this next year. Of course, I have quickly adopted the weeding practices of the people of the Lower Colorado, much to the dismay of my gardening partner! Weeding only twice during the year seems such a sensible thing to do.

Carol's discussion of "acceptance" gardening, a term that she has coined, has given me renewed interest in, and a sense of pride for, the Ojibwa ways of gardening. This year for the first time in a long while I have harvested the fruit of the wild blueberry *(Vaccinium)*, the choke cherry *(Prunus virginiana)*, and the grains of the sacred ma-no-min, also known as wild rice *(Zizania aquatica)*.

As I write this, my attention is broken by the call of a crow. I gaze out the window of my study to see brother crow sitting on a wire high above our garden. Sister corn is gone now, but squash and beans are still there, ripening in the September sun. And so I am reminded once again that the traditions continue. *Brother Crow, Sister Corn* is truly a gift to native people and to all those who enjoy gardening, be it for sustenance, spiritual fulfillment, or for both.

—John Albert Koepke
Saint Paul, Minnesota

ACKNOWLEDGMENTS

No book is ever a single-handed project, and this one is no exception. I am grateful for the people who generously shared their information and expertise when I was researching *Brother Crow, Sister Corn*.

Carol B. Brandt allowed me to read her 1992 paper delivered to the Society of Ethnobiology in March 1992.

Kevin Dahl, Education Director of Native Seeds/SEARCH, helped out with introductions and information materials regarding the work of NS/S.

Jim Enote, Director, Zuni Conservation Project; Andy Laathy, Director, Zuni Sustainable Agriculture Project, and Fred Bowannie, Assistant Director, took time from their busy work day to show me how the Zuni people have adapted centuries-old gardening techniques to modern times in their desert environment.

Roxanne Hamilton graciously allowed me to read her master's thesis, which first showed me the spiritual connection between American Indian gardens and the Beyond.

Loleen Hathaway, Ph.D., Curator of the Navajo Nation Botanical Park and Zoo, described to me some of the difficulties encountered in gardening above seven thousand feet.

Janet Hevey, Assistant Curator, Wheelwright Museum of the American Indian, let me search through the museum's collection of slides for the sand painting of the bears' cave that is reproduced in this book.

Laura Holt, of the Museum of New Mexico, was helpful

regarding the ancient tradition of American Indian gardening.

Joyce Justice, Researcher of the National Archives and Records Administration, in Seattle, was of great assistance in tracking down photographs and reports from the extension services of the 1920s and 1930s.

Robert Klink of the Bureau of Indian Affairs furnished a list of all of the BIA offices throughout the nation.

John Koepke's moral support and encouragement have been invaluable.

Toby Langen pointed out the existence of a gardening project in the 1920s and 1930s on the Tulalip Tribes Reservation. She referred me to Mrs. Ella Stubbs, who kindly wrote me a letter describing her experiences.

Denise Masayesva invited me to the Home Dance at Hotevilla and introduced me to her grandmother, who described how she raised garden plants on the slope of Third Mesa.

Lynn Pankonin, Curator of the Native American collection, Cheney Cowles Museum, Spokane, Washington, described the camas dig she had observed, and offered the resources of the museum's Native American library for research.

Harry Tom described how the gardening program at the Navajo Nation is restoring some ancient traditions and knowledge to the people, besides making use of modern technology.

Finally, my deepest thanks go to Richard Buchanan, for his unstinting moral support and practical help with all the technical computing problems that arise for the writer these days.

INTRODUCTION

THE USUAL IMAGE OF North American Indians has been formed by succeeding generations of European immigrants and their descendants according to the mood of their times. At one point, with the poem "Hiawatha" to remind them, Europeans thought of the Indians living in the Northeastern forests alternatively as "noble savages" or simply "savages." Prior to 1876 and again by the 1930s, the Sioux were thought of romantically as hard-riding, fierce people who lived by their skill with horses and by killing buffalo. After Custer's defeat, the Sioux were murderers. Once memory had faded, they were romanticized in movies. No movies were ever made of the Indians of California or of the lower Great Basin. They were contemptuously referred to as "digger" Indians because they dug for various kinds of roots, their principal foods. The Apache of the Southwest gained a reputation as being exceptionally cruel to their enemies, a reputation they shared with the Kiowa, who lived near what is now Kansas. Lately, all Indians have been cast in the role of victim.

The truth of any people is impossibly complex for one book. This book has only a modest goal—to shed some light on an important activity that has been relatively neglected in favor of spirituality, myths, and suffering. That activity is gardening.

Very seldom have American Indians been portrayed as people who did simple, basic things in order to live. They hunted, fished, gathered, and gardened. Besides growing more than half their food, some people were so successful at gardening that they had enough left over not only to trade but to give away to visitors and the poor. In many places, this trade for garden produce formed the basis of a thriving economy. And like gardeners everywhere, Indians loved their gardens. They decorated them, held festivals in them, and socialized in them. They probably brightened dark days in their winter camps by planning next summer's garden.

Unlike gardeners everywhere, however, their gardens were central to their religions. The corn they planted was not only a crop to eat; it was Mother Corn, or Sister Corn, and was fraught with spiritual significance. Some believed that corn had come with the first people; others believed that the first people were descended from it. Either way, gardening connected them with the earth in ways unknown to most non–Indian gardeners. This book hopes to make that connection clear.

Two major events in the history of American Indians drastically affected their way of life. One was the acquisition of the horse, and the other was the coming of Europeans. The horse gave people freedom and mobility, and greater access to meat. Instead of driving the buffalo herds in a wholesale slaughter over cliffs, men rode alongside the herds and shot individual animals. With the horse, the people could travel greater distances more quickly in search of game. The horse replaced the dog as primary beast of burden.

The arrival of Europeans was not so beneficial. From the beginning, Europeans owed to the Indians their very survival. Had it not been for Squanto's legendary gift of corn and instructions for planting it in hills with a dead fish, the Pilgrims would not have survived their first winter. As Europeans moved westward, they continued to depend on the Indians' sources of food, including garden produce, for which they traded goods the Indians valued.

Unfortunately, they also brought smallpox and other diseases that the Indians' immune systems could not combat. Epidemics changed life for the Indians as radically as had the coming of the horse. The three related branches of Hidatsa moved into the same village to augment their numbers after the smallpox epidemic of 1782 decimated them. After the epidemic of 1834, they entered into a treaty arrangement with the Mandans, who had been similarly affected. The two groups then formed an alliance against their common enemies, most notably, the other branches of the Sioux.

Any description of American Indian gardening must also acknowledge that the American government used agriculture as a weapon against the Indians. Forcing them to live on reservations and exterminating the buffalo, government policy, as enacted in the Dawes Act of 1887, sought to destroy the Plains Indians' nomadic and communal culture and economy, and turn them into sedentary farmers on the European model of single-family farms with an individual allotment of land. Primarily nomadic tribes such as the Cheyenne and the Sioux (who had also been allies at the Battle of the Little Big Horn), were nearly wiped out by starvation. Allotments were especially disastrous for people such as the Assiniboine, whose religion teaches that the earth is their mother; to put a plow in the ground is the same as carving open their human mother's flesh.

Even among those Indians who had already established patterns of life based at least partially on gardening, government policy seriously interfered. The Hidatsa lived in a village from which they daily walked to the gardens. The gardens became sources of community life; young men visited their sweethearts, the women chatted and sang to each other as they worked or watched over the gardens.

After imposing reservation boundaries on them, the government for a time allowed them to continue living in the village. Then, noting that the village was becoming a haven for disreputable types who were selling white lightning (corn liquor) to the Indians, each family was given an allotment of land to farm for themselves. The village was destroyed; dwellings were leveled. The government provided tools and farm implements, and being gardeners already, with no prejudices or religious taboos against the work, the Hidatsa more or less succeeded as farmers, in contrast to many other tribes. Unfortunately, however, gardening had never been the province of men, who were now robbed of their hunting and protective role in life, and farming European-style was beyond the strength of many women. The Hidatsa, and others, resented the destruction of their community.

Eventually, seeing that the allotment system was a disaster for Indians, the government abandoned the policy. Yet in 1982, forty-seven hundred Indians owned their own farms, and more than 60 percent were employed in agriculture in some capacity.

Today, there has been a resurgence of Indian self-reliance that has been reflected in a number of large gardening associations, particularly the Navajo New Dawn Project (page 112). People are becoming more self-sufficient as they learn about their ancient gardening traditions and techniques—techniques that were developed over centuries and that really work. There is still much to be learned, and I hope that this book sparks interest toward further research and understanding.

1
THE AMERICAN INDIAN WAY OF GARDENING

Near the beginning of time, Kakh, Brother Crow, brought to the people seeds of all sorts, especially corn, to nourish and replenish them. And the people cultivated their gardens so that when game was scarce they did not go hungry. Because Sister Corn gives of herself that they might live, the people return thanks to her in songs and ceremonies at planting time and at harvest.

So the Yuma tell the story of how Sister Corn came to them from Brother Crow. Corn or maize figures in many American Indian myths of the beginning of people on earth. The traditions of native people who gardened teach that corn came to them from a super-natural being, but each tribe had its own version of which being gave them this essential food. The Omaha say that of all the other beings, only Crow helped them get their human form when they

5

were nebulous spirits, formless and longing for shape. Then with form came hunger, and Wakonda, the Creator, gave them corn to fill their bellies. Seneca myths tell how their Creator put the Three Sisters (corn, beans, and squash) on earth for the benefit of the people, and directed the people to always include them in their ceremonies.

The Cheyenne received both corn and bison from Great Medicine, the creator of the earth. The Pawnee maintain that the Father gave them corn, squash, and beans. Both the Penobscot of New England and the Hopi of the Southwest tell how the Corn Mother gave the people life. The Navajo believe that corn was among the First Ones, and that First Man and First Woman were created from two ears of corn, the white ear and the yellow ear. The First Ones sing:

> From below the earth my corn comes
> I walk with you.
> From above the water for the young comes
> I walk with you.
> From above vegetation comes to the earth
> I walk with you.
> From below the earth corn pollen comes
> I walk with you.

For many gardening people, the connection between cultivated vegetables, particularly corn, and themselves is so close as to be flesh of flesh. Human life is bought with sacrifice and sealed with the life of the corn plant, as it is with the lives of the deer, bison, or salmon. No matter which foods the various tribes depended on, they understood this to be truth.

The Cherokee tell of Selu, the Corn Mother, who with her husband Kana'ti, the Lucky Hunter, existed before the people. Prior to each meal, Selu would disappear and return with a bowl of corn kernels. Disobeying her orders not to do so, her sons followed her

BROTHER CROW, SISTER CORN

to see how she got this food, and to their horror saw her shake the kernels from her body into the bowl. Believing her to be a witch, they killed her. Before she died, she gave them instructions on how to treat her corpse. In this way, the death of Selu gave the people corn, for she was resurrected after death as a corn plant.

When people eat the vegetables that grow in their gardens, the substance of the plants joins with the substance of the person in a way that is more than physical—more than the survival of the body. It is a survival of the spirit, also. The people's spirits also meet the spirits of the Corn Mother, or the Three Sisters, who give of their flesh to ensure the survival of the people.

The role of the crow in the Yuma myth symbolizes the human relationship with other living beings. Often, a bird is associated with the gift of corn to the people. For the White Mountain Apache, the turkey brings corn to the people and teaches them how to plant it. The Mandan believed that the Old Woman Who Never Dies kept the gardens through the winter on the island in the south where she lived. In the spring, she sent her messengers, the big birds—wild geese and ducks and crows—north to signal the planting season. Sioux belief is typical of the kinship most native peoples felt with the natural world: people are "a living part of the natural world, brother and sister to the grain and the trees, the bison and the bear." This sense of kinship carried over into hunting and gardening.

When men hunted, they often sang prayer songs to the game animals—primarily the deer and the bison. These songs asked for the animals' cooperation prior to the hunt. A Navajo might pray, "Brother Deer, come to me and give me your flesh that my family might live." Afterward, they asked for the animals' forgiveness for the taking of their lives, and thanked them for making the supreme sacrifice for the people's well-being. The spirits of the plants were likewise persuaded to give up their physical existence for the sake of the people. Similar songs to garden crops thank the beans, corn, and squash for the gifts of their substance. These songs exist wherever people gardened, from the Navajo in modern-day Arizona to the Seneca in modern-day New York.

At planting, gardeners invoked other spirits to protect the crops from drought, flood, and pests, and to give them a good harvest. They sang songs to the corn to encourage it to grow. Here is one such Mandan song:

My daughter is
This corn.
I can never use it up.

When harvest came, and with it the assurance that they would not starve that year, people gave thanks. The Iroquois prayed: "We return thanks to the corn, and to her sisters, the beans and squashes, which give us life."

Traditional American Indian gardens are alive not just as all gardens are alive, with plants sprouting, but with spiritual life—all living things are spiritually related. The traditional Indian way of gardening therefore involves much more than seed selection, gardening techniques, close observation of plants, and knowledge of local climate, soil, and weather conditions. These elements are crucial to the success of native gardens, as they are to any garden, but the Indian way of gardening involves spiritualism as well. A variety of spirits influenced the gardens and had to be persuaded to join the side of the people. In times of drought, rain had to be reminded that the gardens needed water. It had to be persuaded to fall. The spirits of pests such as the grasshopper and sometimes the crow had to be convinced to stay away from the gardens. Gardening contained this spiritual element because it was vital to their survival and occupied a central place in their culture. Cultivating vegetables was for many tribes an activity that formed the basis of their culture, art, and social and religious life. The gardening year, to a large degree, determined the ceremonial year.

Planting rituals asked for the spirits' help in growing a good crop. When the plants ripened, people celebrated with thanksgiving ceremonials to the spirits. Nearly everyone who grew corn held Green Corn celebrations in late July or early August when the corn was first ready for picking. The Green Corn ritual of the Hidatsa went on for four days, and like most other Green Corn ceremonials was a time for relaxing from the difficult, anxious labors of finding food. The Corn Dances of the Santo Domingo Pueblo near Santa Fe are still celebrated every August 4, on Saint Dominic's day. Some ceremonies held around the time of the winter solstice, such as those observed by the Seneca and Zuni, aimed at getting the new gardening year off to the proper start by aligning the people and the spirits toward the same purpose: having enough to eat.

Agriculture and horticulture have always been tricky endeavors. Not every year or every garden yields a bountiful crop. Gardeners defy floods, drought, late (or early) freezes, or pests, and can only hope that despite everything they will produce enough food. When Indian gardens did not succeed against any of these ills, many blamed themselves for having failed to please the spirits. Something in their ceremonial observances had not been right. Their attitudes had not been completely believing, or they had erred in the construction of an altar or in the chant of a ritual.

🌲 Types of Gardening 🌲

In addition to hunting or fishing, American Indians practiced two kinds of gardening. In one, they cultivated vegetables or tobacco for food, religious purposes, and trade. They planted the seeds, hoed perhaps once or twice in the growing season, harvested the crop, and selected the best seed for the next year. This type of gardening was recognizable to immigrants, as it resembled their own methods of gardening. The other type, however, works in harmony with the bounty of nature. Indians harvested native plants and put back enough seed, or left enough plants, to make certain that there would be an adequate supply of food the following year. This type of gardening might be called acceptance gardening. It accepts what nature provides and uses human means to ensure a future of plenty. This was the most widespread method by the native peoples. Those who did not grow vegetables gathered seeds or dug roots. Wherever people cultivated gardens, they also practiced acceptance gardening because life was too precarious to depend solely on one mode of food production. Here too they invoked the aid of the spirits. When the berries ripened, most people performed ceremonies of thanksgiving for first fruits. When they dug the tubers of the Jerusalem artichoke or the camas, they took care to ceremonially plant the seeds.

⚘ WHO GARDENED, AND WHERE ⚘

One or both of these kinds of gardening can be found in all eight of the culture areas in the contiguous United States (see page 86). A culture area is a geographic section of the continent in which the people had similar patterns of living. Although there were often large differences from tribe to tribe and sometimes from band to band, the climate, together with available water and game animals, caused people to develop similar coping mechanisms in order to survive.

West of the Mississippi, except for coastal and mountainous regions, the continent is arid; eastward, water is more abundant. Bison, in the west, ranged far in search of grass; deer, a primary foodsource in the east, found more food within a more limited area. Consequently, most of the people who depended on bison developed a nomadic way of life. The bison hunters might also cultivate tobacco or vegetables, but compared to the eastern tribes, relatively few of these gardeners lived in settled towns where they could spend much time weeding the gardens and devoting a major part of the season to cultivating them. The Hidatsa were among these few, as were some Sioux bands—stereotypes portray them as nomadic, fierce fighters, and superb horsemen. Yet among the numerous bands of Sioux were the Santee and the Mandan peoples, who were famous gardeners. Lewis and Clark traded for vegetables with the Mandan and the Hidatsa on their way west in 1804. In fact, the Hidatsa, themselves great gardeners, said they learned to garden from the Mandan people.

Some Plains bands, such as the Oglalla and Teton Sioux or the Cheyenne, might pack up whole villages and travel about in search of bison, returning to their winter encampment sites to wait out the snows. To provide themselves with vegetables, these people often needed to trade or raid for them. But the Hidatsa and the Mandan depended on vegetable gardening to provide more than half of their subsistence and economy. These and other people, such as their southern neighbors, the Pawnee, the Kiowa, and the Arapaho, all produced enough vegetables for themselves and for trade with peoples who did not garden. Even the Cheyenne, noted horsemen and nongardeners, believed they began as gardeners, according to this story:

One day, a young man went out to hunt, but he had no luck. It was near the beginning of the world, and there was not much to eat. He was very thirsty, tired, and discouraged when he stopped to drink at a spring. Seeing him near despair, and faint for lack of food, the Old Woman Who Lives In A Spring took pity on him. "Go south," she said, "and you will find plenty of meat, for the bison live there." The young man traveled south, and just as the Old Woman had said, there was plenty of meat. Later, this man happened to meet another young man who had also been instructed by the same woman. "Go north," she had told the second young man. He had journeyed to the north, and there he found corn. When the two young men discovered each other, they combined their treasures and the people had plenty to eat.

After the Cheyenne migrated to the Great Plains and acquired the horse, they followed the buffalo more, and rarely gardened. The Osage, on the other hand, continued to garden after they obtained horses. Like many of the bison-hunters, they planted their corn and other crops in the spring, left to hunt bison in mid-summer, and returned in mid September for the harvest. After harvest, and after the meat was dried and the skins cured in autumn, they moved away from the summer village to the winter encampment. The Blackfeet and the Crow, also Plains people, developed complex social and religious structures around tobacco gardening. Their Tobacco Societies conducted elaborate ceremonies designed to enlist the spirits' help with the tobacco crop.

Along the shores of Lake Erie, tribes such as the Seneca (one of the members of the Iroquois Confederation) hunted deer, gathered berries and maple syrup, and grew vegetables and tobacco in well-tended plots. In what is now New England, Potawatomi men went on deer-hunting expeditions while the women and older people stayed behind to tend the gardens. Early observers of the Lenni Lenape (from modern-day Delaware) found that gardening was the foundation of their economy. It attached the people to the soil during the growing seasons, although the quest for food and clothing necessitated their moving back and forth at certain seasons. The principal crops were corn, beans, pumpkins, squash, and tobacco.

In what is now Minnesota's arrowhead region, the Ojibwa hunted deer, fished, harvested wild rice (*Zinzania aquatica*) and cultivated vegetables and tobacco. In the southeastern woodlands, people living in the present states of Georgia, Alabama, and Mississippi had extensive plots of vegetables. Together with the Seminoles of Florida, the Cherokee, Choctaw, Creek, and Chickasaw had such settled, agricultural societies that they became known as the Five Civilized Tribes. They continued this gardening tradition even after their forced removal to Oklahoma.

In the desert Southwest, a place that Europeans considered pretty much uninhabitable, native people raised vegetables, hunted

LEFT
*Indian corn in
the garden of the
Zuni Sustainable
Agriculture Project
(see pages 112–116).
Zuni, New Mexico.*

CAROL BUCHANAN

BOTTOM
*Model waffle garden at the
Ashiwi Awan Museum
and Heritage Center.
Zuni, New Mexico.*

CAROL BUCHANAN

Elders of the Tobacco Society mix the seed with elk manure.

Members of the Tobacco Society prepare the ground.

meat, and traded with other tribes for what they could not produce. The Hopi, for example, lived (and still live) in adobe houses in permanent towns. They gardened at seven thousand feet above sea level—on top of the mesas where their towns were situated or in secluded, walled, terraced plots scraped out of the cliff face.

The semiarid Great Basin, between the Rockies and the Sierra Nevadas, has always been among the least-populated parts of the United States. Here, the Shoshoni, the Utes, and other people eked out a living by gathering roots and berries, hunting, and trapping small animals and insects. If they lived near a spring or a reliable stream, they grew vegetables to supplement what they could not get by gathering seeds.

The people on the western slopes of the Sierra ranges seem to have pursued vegetable gardening more in the south than in the north, but around Mount Shasta, the Karok, the Yurok, and other people based their society and their economy on the cultivation of tobacco and a moneylike medium of exchange.

The Nez Percé and the Walla Walla, from the arid flatlands of the Columbia and Snake watersheds in eastern Washington and Oregon, forged a system of trade whose two major commodities were salmon and camas bulbs (*Camassia quamash*). This bulb was an important source of nutrients, and its sweet taste made it popular everywhere it was known. Both the Walla Walla and the Nez Percé established trade relationships and routes east to the Plains tribes and south into California. Camas was as important to the Plateau people as wild rice was to the Ojibwa, and both groups practiced acceptance gardening extensively, with all the proper ceremonial observances to encourage the spirits to continue giving the people these natural crops.

The Northern Kutenai occupied the mountain fastnesses of the Rockies of northern Idaho, northwestern Montana, and southern Alberta. Like the Crow and the Blackfeet, they developed a significant culture around tobacco. They hunted deer and other game, and gathered roots and berries, but traded for their other needs—for camas with Plateau people, and for corn with the Plains people.

The people of the Northwest Coast were among the more fortunate of native people in that they lived in an area so abundant in vegetable products, berries, and fish that their gardening was confined to such activities as burning off the forests so that huckleberries would grow. They developed cultures around trade and ocean fishing, including whaling. The Makah, a whaling people, still live on the westernmost corner of Washington State, where the Pacific Ocean and the Strait of Juan de Fuca meet. The Chinook, who lived at the mouth of the Columbia, dominated Indian trade in the Pacific Northwest.

🌲 THE GARDENS 🌲

Universally, the main crops of an American Indian garden were corn, beans, and squash—the Three Sisters of the Iroquois; the American trio of garden vegetables. Depending on their climate and culture, Indians also produced foods such as turnips, tomatoes, and sunflowers. These cultivated gardens varied greatly in appearance. Sometimes they resembled their European counterparts in that they were well defined and fenced, both to protect the plants from predators and to mark off individual plots. Sometimes the gardens were hidden among the forest plants, so that a passerby might or might not see a corn plant or a bush bean sprouting among the woodland ferns.

Women nearly always grew the vegetables, while men grew tobacco, hunted or fished, and protected the women and children. With only the shoulder blade of a bison or deer to work with, a gardener could not work a very large plot. Because individual plots were small and the need could be great, gardening was intensive. The Seneca planted beans and corn together in hills, so the corn stalks could support the bean vines. A plot perhaps an eighth of an acre could yield enough to support a family for a year, provide produce for trade, and leave enough to feed visitors. Some, but not all, tribes maintained communal gardens. The Creeks had communal plots of about twenty acres, which everyone helped with. Whether the gardens were individual or communal, Indians were generous with their produce—up to a point. The Mandan might give their produce freely to visitors, but at the same time, to keep from being eaten out of house and home, they passed along rumors that enemies were in the neighborhood.

Plains gardeners followed various practices that combined tending the garden with hunting bison. The Hidatsa and Mandan remained in the summer village and hunted bison within range. After the Blackfeet had planted their tobacco, except for checking on it once or twice during the bison hunt, they left it in the hands of the spirits until they returned to harvest it. Even with such haphazard cultivation, the gardens could yield a good crop when conditions were right. This method may have worked because the species of tobacco was a native plant. Less rather than more cultivation is often the better approach for gardening with indigenous plants.

Once people had harvested their crops, they had to find a way of storing them for the next year. Each group devised a method of storage that satisfied the conditions in their local area. Those who remained in the same place throughout the year did not concern themselves so much with predators finding their produce in their absence as with the elements. Some Southern people constructed storage places above ground to protect them from high water. Plains people who left a summer encampment and settled elsewhere for the winter contrived well-disguised, hidden caches that protected their vegetables from predators (human and animal) and from the elements. Usually these caches were buried and the openings hidden with turf. It was a disaster when the people returned home from a hunt or from the winter encampment in the spring to find their caches looted. There would be no more corn until the next harvest, sometimes months away.

☽ THE POSITION OF WOMEN ☾

Although generally, among tribes that gardened, men hunted and women tended the gardens, everyone seems to have pitched in where good sense indicated. Men did the heavy work and women did the lighter work, according to their strength. Occasionally, early travelers recorded that a man loved his wife so much that he helped her with the planting or hoeing, but this seems to be more an exception than a rule. For the Fox Indians, who were originally a people of the Northern Woodlands, roles were clearly defined. William Jones, a Fox Indian, wrote about his people:

> It was the duty of men to hunt, fight, build lodges, dig canoes, take care of the horses, make wooden spoons, etc. The women were to hew wood, carry water, plant and raise corn, take care of their families, and in the absence of the men, attend to the horses, build the lodges, etc.

Varying degrees of dependence on garden crops influenced the position of women among the tribes. Among the Blackfeet, who cultivated only tobacco, the position of women was less equal than among gardening tribes such as the Mandan, the Osage, or the Seneca. Among these people, gardening ranked equally with hunting as a strategy for survival, and the position of women was one of equality. Food products, both meat and vegetables, were also important trade commodities throughout Indian America. Here, too, women played a dominant part, for among gardening people they supplied half of the trade goods. Acceptance gardeners on the Plateau, such as the Nez Percé, Walla Walla, or Shoshoni women, dug camas bulbs and made them into sweet cakes that were considered delicacies and widely traded. Early European travelers noted that women were often sharp traders. It was not easy to get the better of people who lived by produce and trade, and if it was done once, they remembered the next time. In consequence, the price of produce often rose when less desirable customers came back for more.

Being responsible for half the group's economic welfare gave women power. And put them in danger. It was a situation European observers sometimes misinterpreted. Seeing women hard at work in the gardens while able-bodied men appeared to lounge about the village, or younger men hung around the gardens flirting with eligible girls (under the watchful eyes of their mothers), some Europeans assumed that a great inequality existed between men and women. Not so. Actually, the men were on guard, protecting the gardens and the women who gardened. A man who is occupied is not watchful. For it was a sad fact of Indian life that constant watchfulness against enemies was necessary. It was not unusual for women to be attacked and sometimes murdered in their gardens by enemies of the tribe or raiders after food. The people lived lives of constant watchfulness, and a man busy at some chore could find himself or his family murdered before he could drop a tool and pick up a weapon. In 1810, Alexander Henry, the Northwest Company fur trader, found an armed guard at a Mandan garden. Nearly a hundred years later, an observer reported that among the Pima, women were the gardeners because they were so constantly harassed by their enemies that Pima men could not safely lay aside their bows during any waking moment.

Hunting was not a matter of an hour here or there. A man out hunting for deer meat to feed his family might be gone several days or longer. In the forests, although trails existed, game obviously didn't always use them. In the pursuit of deer or elk, a man struggled over fallen timbers, through dense undergrowth, and waded in cold, treacherous streams. He was constantly on the lookout for human predators, especially as he carried hundreds of pounds of meat home on his back. Bison hunting on the Plains involved packing up everything and following the migrating herds wherever they led. Women went along to help prepare the skins and the meat, but it was the men's work to hunt the animals and protect the encampment from enemies.

Gardening as the Foundation of Trade

The economics of Indian life was based on hunting and gardening, both of which in turn supported trade. Native people improved their existence by trading (or raiding) for what they could not grow, hunt, or make. And produce, whether camas, the American trio, or tobacco, was central in this trade. Some Plains people, such as the Crow and the Blackfeet, might grow only tobacco but trade for vegetables with others, such as the Mandan. The Crow and the Blackfeet also traded for camas with the Nez Percé, who rode across the Rockies to trade. They and the Walla Walla also traded southward into California and the Great Basin. In the southern Plains, the Comanche traded their bison meat and hides for corn and other vegetables grown by the people of the eastern Pueblos of New Mexico. The gardening tribes established patterns of trade with people who did less gardening. In exchange for their produce, the gardeners gained items of value to them—eagle feathers, horses, bison robes. As Europeans moved westward, they also became involved in this trade. From Europeans themselves, or indirectly from people who were in frequent contact with them, gardeners acquired commodities such as guns, powder and shot, iron kettles, awls, and garden tools.

In some cultures, the cultivation of tobacco *(Nicotiana)*was as important or more so than growing vegetables. It held a vital place in the worship of all American Indian people. It carried prayers to the spirits, and in itself it made a pleasing offering. Because it was so universally smoked, tobacco was valued throughout Indian America as a trade commodity. Nearly every group or tribe seems to have had its own recipe of enhancements to make it taste better, or to induce a floating state of mind that was receptive to spirit messages. Wherever people met, they were always eager to try someone else's blend and trade for it if they liked the effects. In the southwest, the Yuma and the Pima (who got it from the Papago) grew *N.*

trigonophylla; on the northern Plains, the Crow cultivated *N. multivalvis* and *N. quadrivalvis*. Coyote tobacco (*N. bigelovii*), was grown by the Karok in northern California, and "under-the-creosote-bush" tobacco *(N. attenuata)* was grown throughout the Southwest. The most widely distributed species, *N. rustica*, was found throughout the eastern half of the North American continent from Hudson's Bay to the Gulf of Mexico. In smoking, the pure tobacco leaf was often mixed with local herbs, such as kinnickinnick (*Arctostaphylos urva-ursi* in Montana and the Pacific Northwest) or its relatives (*A. pulchella* in the Southwest), which gave a different flavor to the tobacco of one group than would be found in the tobacco smoked by other people.

⚘ THE DEBT ⚘

The typical modern American Thanksgiving dinner includes a menu of roast turkey, cranberries, yams, potatoes, corn, beans, squash, and pumpkin pie. All of these foods originated here, and subsequent immigrants to these shores owe American Indians the debt of survival, a debt commemorated at Thanksgiving with these indigenous American foods. But we're certainly not the only ones to owe so much to Indian gardening. In Azerbaijan, on the eastern shore of the Caspian Sea, cornfields stretch across the land. Ireland is famous for its dependence on the potato. A Russian breakfast often includes piroschkies, pastries made of a potato dough wrapped around a meat or jam filling. And on several continents, seed catalogs arriving in gardeners' mailboxes include colorful varieties of "Indian corn" recommended for popping and decoration, and hundreds of varieties of hybrid sweet corn. No matter what it is now called, all corn originally came from Indian corn. Without American Indian gardeners, much of the world's cuisine would be different.

2

CROPS, TECHNIQUES, AND RELIGION

When Europeans arrived in what would become America, more than two hundred tribes were growing their own vegetables. Traveling through the present upstate New York in 1605, Sieur de Champlain remarked on the beautiful Seneca gardens where abundant crops of the Three Sisters, pumpkins, and tobacco were growing in cultivated plots in the Genesee Valley. In 1775, naturalist William Bartram, traveling through what is now Georgia and Alabama, commented on the Creeks' gardens of corn, rice, beans, all the species of *Cucurbits*—squashes, pumpkins, and watermelons—and those nourishing roots usually called sweet potatoes (the Creek confederacy never planted or ate the Irish potato). When all went well, in seasons with enough water, few or no pests, and no surprise frosts, Indian gardeners could feed themselves and their families well, contribute to the maintenance of the poor, and have an excess for trade. When all did not go well, they were on the brink of starvation.

✳ WHAT THEY GREW ✳

As Champlain, Bartram and other travelers noted, throughout the land people cultivated the basic three food plants: corn *(Zea mays)*, beans *(Phaseolus)*, and squash *(Cucurbita)*. Other indigenous crops included cotton, peanuts, tomatoes, lima beans, melons, peas, sunflowers (especially the Jerusalem artichoke), marsh elder *(Iva annua)*, knotweed *(Polygonum)*, goosefoot *(Chenopodium)*, and pigweed *(Amaranth)*. The Kutenai had such extensive tobacco gardens that the area where they grew tobacco is still called Tobacco Plains. David Douglas, the noted Scottish plant hunter whose name identifies the Douglas fir, discovered a tobacco garden in the North Pacific Coast region in 1827. He had traveled fifty miles upstream along the Willamette River (in present-day western Oregon) when he beached his canoe to hunt for plants on the shore. Not far away, he discovered a little garden of tobacco of a species unknown to Europeans. Congratulating himself, Douglas happily collected some seeds and plants, and was on his way back to camp when he met the unhappy gardener. Douglas described the meeting in his journal: "The owner, seeing [the plants] under my arm, appeared to be much displeased; but by presenting him with two finger-lengths of tobacco from Europe his wrath was appeased, and we became good friends." Douglas paid with tobacco both for the plants and for information. The gardener told Douglas much about the growth and cultivation of tobacco, and about conditions along the river. They parted with each man seemingly pleased with his end of the bargain. Although the various species of tobacco were found wild nearly everywhere, most people preferred to grow their own. Some people did so because of beliefs about wild tobacco. The Karok, for example, would not smoke wild tobacco because the seed could have fallen on a burial ground and been contaminated by the dead.

Not all of the Indians' garden plants were indigenous. Once gardeners liked an imported plant, they very quickly adapted it

BROTHER CROW, SISTER CORN

into their gardens and their diets. Watermelons, for example, are not native to the Western Hemisphere, but when a Spanish priest and explorer named Father Kino first met the Yuma at the confluence of the Gila and Lower Colorado rivers in 1701, he found them already growing this fruit, whose juice was a welcome treat during the long heat of summer. Traded from hand to hand, the seeds had traveled faster than the Church. Navajo gardeners today consider chiles, not originally native to the region, to be one of their four basic crops, along with corn, beans, and squash.

⚘ GARDENING CONDITIONS ⚘

Native people used organic gardening methods in widely varying conditions, from the high deserts of the southwest, to the woodlands of New York, to the steamy heat of the Southeast. On the northern Plains, the Mandan and the Hidatsa became famous for their produce, although they gardened in one of the harshest climate zones of the country—Missouri River valley in North Dakota. After smallpox nearly wiped them out in the late eighteenth century, these two allied tribes joined forces as protection from enemies. They lived in towns on the bluffs above the upper Missouri river, but planted their gardens along the river bottoms in good soil rather than trying to plant in the dry, hard soil of the prairie with their digging sticks and hoes made of bison bones. This is the northernmost latitude where corn will mature. It requires 70 to 120 days from germination until maturity. The growing season in this area is 90 to 120 days, and annual rainfall is less than ten inches. Winter temperatures can drop to thirty or forty degrees below zero, and summer temperatures can soar over a hundred. In such conditions, these tribes were able to grow only a few secondary crops besides the American trio, primarily sunflowers *(Helianthus annua)* and pumpkins. Even so, they were generally so successful that their villages became trading centers for vegetables; the Cheyenne, Sioux, Assiniboine, Crow, and Blackfeet came from hundreds of miles to barter for their produce. Lewis and Clark, and other explorers, stopped there to trade for corn, beans, and squash.

The high humidity and high annual rainfall of the Midwest could cause crops to rot in the ground, making it difficult to keep stored food. People of the desert Southwest had the opposite problem: lack of rainfall. The high deserts receive an average annual rainfall of only nine to twelve inches. Gardening at seven thousand feet above sea level means coping with a growing season of 90–120 days, alkaline soil, constant dessicating wind, and temperature swings of forty to fifty degrees in one day. Yet the Zuni (New Mexico), Hopi (Arizona), and others made that high, arid region a food basket. A late-nineteenth-century list of Hopi crops included: corn, beans, squash, watermelons, muskmelons, onions, gourds, chiles, sunflowers, wheat, sorghum, tomatoes, potatoes, cotton, grapes, pumpkins, garlic, coriander, saffron, tobacco, peaches, apricots, nectarines, and tobacco. Many of these crops are still grown by traditional methods.

For the people of southern California and Arizona, along the lower Colorado river, the only reliable source of water for gardens was the river's annual overflow. Working at sea level, where temperatures commonly reach above a hundred in the summer, the Mohave, Yuma, and other people grew corn, beans, and squash, along with tobacco and gourds. These last made excellent storage vessels for corn and other crops, and as water canteens. Lack of reliable water was not necessarily a problem along the Lower Colorado and Gila rivers, even though rainfall was (and remains) minimal and sparse. In the early twentieth century, rainfall averaged approximately three-and-a-half to five inches, combined with wide swings in temperatures, from a high of 127 degrees to a low of 14 or less. However, in overflowing its banks every spring, the river dumped both water and fresh soil in the form of silt. Immediately after the water receded enough to plant, people placed their seeds in large holes dug deeply into the silt—perhaps a foot—and covered it lightly. As the plant grew, the gardeners filled in more of the hole. Eventually, the plant was tall enough to mound soil around the stalk or vine at the surface. When the soil dried, either the garden was ready for harvest, or they brought water to it. The Cocopa, who lived farthest south on the river in Mexico, built a system of dams, levees, and ditches to channel water. Farther north, the Mohave carried water in ollas, large containers made from gourds they grew in their gardens. Elsewhere, in the high deserts, people gardened wherever they could find water or carry water to the gardens. In Arizona, some of the Navajo raised their crops at the bottoms of deep canyons such as the Grand Canyon or Canyon de Chelly, where they could take advantage of annual floods. Other Navajo, like the Hopi, gardened above the canyons and depended on erratic rainfalls or natural springs. The Zuni drew their water from what is now Nutria Lake, from springs, and on the sacred mesa Towa Yalanne (Corn Mountain). To ensure that they would have enough water for the gardens, people developed various techniques, some practical and some spiritual. One method was to irrigate or carry water for long distances. The other was to convince the spirits to help out by bringing rain.

In a group of terraced Hopi gardens, people still use traditional techniques for irrigation. These gardens climb the steep slope of Third Mesa, below the town of Hotevilla. A waist-high wall of the pale blond stone encloses each garden, a space perhaps ten by twelve feet. Here, some gardeners grow the Hopi basic four (corn, beans, squash, and chile peppers), along with tomatoes and sunflowers. Their deep-green foliage contrasts with and softens the golden stone walls. The varying foliage provides textural contrasts. Corn leaves arch protectively over the tomatoes, and sunflowers lift their bright yellow flowerheads over the walls. Perhaps because they have not been designed, these gardens lack self-consciousness. Approximately fifty feet above the first gardens, a spring pours fresh water from the mesa. The people have channeled this water into a catch basin. From there, water must be poured into a series of connecting shallow ditches that carry water by gravity to whichever garden needs moisture. A Hopi grandmother says that in her youth she would throw two hundred buckets over the lip of the basin, walk down to see how much more water was needed, then walk up and throw over perhaps two hundred more. She continued this alternating pour-and-climb until the garden was watered.

Irrigation systems were in use along the Rio Grande as long ago as 900 A.D. Some people steered the flow of water into shallow ponds made by banking up the sides with logs and dirt. Others constructed small dams, then channeled the flow where they needed it by means of a series of ditches and levees. When water was wanted in a different part of the garden, they broke open a small section of the levee and stopped up the original channel. The Zuni invented the waffle garden to conserve water in their desert environment. They built up dirt around all four sides of a small rectangle. Each section was two or more square feet, and they added adjoining sections until the entire garden was quite large. There was no standard or optimum size of either the individual section or of the garden as a whole. Within each depression, they planted seeds of several plants. Periodically, they flooded each depression, but let the sides go dry except for the water that wicked upward through the dirt. Where water was scarce, native people took no chances when it came to providing enough rain for their gardens.

Much of Zuni religion is designed to bring water to their desert environment. Water is the Grandfather of all life, as the Sun and the Earth are Father and Mother. The frog is an important fetish to the Zuni, for it represents water. Much prayer and many of the more important ceremonies are designed to bring water to the corn. Envisioning was another technique by which people encouraged the rain (or anything else they wanted to happen). They sang songs that envisioned great rainstorms:

BROTHER CROW, SISTER CORN

Green rock mountains are thundering with clouds.
With this thunder the village is shaking.
The water will come down the arroyo and I will float
     on the water.
Afterwards the corn will ripen in the fields.

Or this one:

A cloud on top of Evergreen Trees Mountain is singing,
A cloud on top of Evergreen Trees Mountain is
     standing still,
It is raining and thundering up there,
It is raining here,
Under the mountain the corn tassels are shaking
Under the mountain the horns of the child corn are glistening.

A climate hospitable to plants is also hospitable to pests. William Bartram found that gardens close to the shores of some rivers were not safe from alligators—and sometimes the gardeners weren't, either. Abundant insect life posed a problem when their eggs hatched and larvae devoured the produce. From the seventeen-year locust or the common grasshopper to deer, birds, and human raiders, pests were a terrible problem. Again, people took both practical and spiritual means to combat them. William Bartram reported that the Creeks posted guards:

> The men patrol the cornfields at night, to protect their provisions from
> the depredations of night rovers, as bears, raccoons, and deer; the two
> former being immoderately fond of young corn, when the grain is filled
> with a rich milk, as sweet and nourishing as cream; and the deer are as
> fond of the potato vines.

When they found too many insects on their plants, the White

Mountain Apache conducted a ceremony designed to bring rain to wash them off. Other Apache groups called in spiritual practitioners who had the power to drive insects from the gardens by singing special songs. Other people resorted to natural insecticides and poisons. One early traveler, Thomas Hariot, reported in 1587 that the Iroquois soaked their seed corn in an herbal decoction of warm water, the roots of one of the *Helleborus* species (probably *Helleborus foetidus*), and another herb he could not identify. The gardeners said the solution was medicine for the corn, but it was really a poison for any bird that ate the seed corn. The bird who ate this corn became punchy, and reeled about in a manner that frightened the others, who, the theory went, would leave the garden.

The idea that animals could communicate with each other on a spirit level gave rise to the Zuni practice of severely punishing an animal or a bird caught stealing their corn. It was felt that if the animal suffered, its spirit would warn the spirits of the others not to steal corn. Frank Cushing, an anthropologist who was adopted into the Zuni tribe in the late nineteenth century, relates the incident of the crow who was caught in the corn patch. The farmer cut off the bird's beak and confined it within reach of a pile of corn, which it could not eat. It starved to death.

⚜ WHO OWNED THE LAND ⚜

Despite some cultural variations among the tribes, the concept of land ownership was basically the same throughout Indian America. Land, like the air and water, was a gift from the spirits, the Great Spirit, the Manitou, or the Maker. Whoever occupied the land owned it, but only temporarily, and the idea that land could be bought or sold, as Europeans believed, was unknown here. Land belonged to all the children to come, and must be passed on to them for their use. That being the case, in some cultures, such as the Iroquois tribes, women owned the land because they bore the children. Generally, a garden was owned by the people who worked in it. As long as a family continued to garden on a piece, no one (of their own or an allied tribe) bothered them or interfered with them. But if they ceased to work a piece of ground for an entire season, the next season it belonged to anyone who wanted to take it.

⚶ Selecting Seeds ⚶

The quality of the garden depends upon the quality of the seeds. Indigenous people thoroughly understood that concept, and they made a point of selecting only the best seeds for the next year's crop. During harvest, people carefully and ceremonially selected seed. Or, if the crop were poor, the gardeners used the seed of an earlier year, which they had kept for emergencies. (Some people kept a three-years' supply of seeds in dry storage.) Close attention to the quality of the seed assured a high rate of germination, but equally important, especially when selecting corn seed, was careful attention to the proper ceremonial requirements. Those crops mattered not only as food that ensured survival, but as part of the sacred, spiritual environment in which they lived. For example, wherever people had sacred associations with colors of corn or beans, they made an effort to keep the different colors pure. They sorted seeds by color, stored them separately, and planted the different colors in separate plots to prevent cross-pollination by the wind or flying insects.

Some people based their seed selection on the vigor of the plant and the ears; others considered primarily the shape and plumpness of the seed kernels. The Western Apache selected eight ceremonial stalks of corn and four ears of female corn. One of these four ears would supply seed. The rest of the seed they took from the choicest plants, generally the largest ears and the tallest stalks. If the seed came from the strongest plants, they reasoned, the crop should be good. The Creeks had different criteria. William Bartram observed that these people regarded good seed, good soil, and cultivation to be of utmost importance in ensuring a good crop. When selecting corn seed, they did not make their selections in the field, from the strongest plants. They paid more attention to the kernels than to the size or shape of the ear, and took special care to save ears with mature, large, plump, well-developed grains. The straightness of the rows on the ears was not important to them, either. They had found that the kernels near the tip of the ear germinated poorly and gave unsatisfactory results, so they threw these out. Tobacco gardeners worked at improving their tobacco to make it different from other people's, or to make it taste better. The Karok tried to breed a different, stronger, tobacco than the wild tobacco by selecting seed from only the strongest-tasting tobaccos in their cultivated plots. By selecting the best seed over a period of years, native people bred plants suitable for local soil and climate conditions.

⁂ CLASSIFICATION ⁂

The native peoples' success in developing different varieties of corn derived from their skill at plant classification. Their survival depended on their being close observers of the plant life around them. This vital experience with plants was passed on to the next generations, who added additional experiences. Plant knowledge snowballed from generation to generation until people were seldom fooled into eating the wrong sort of plant or plant part.

Native people classified plants according to usefulness, good taste, or medicinal qualities. At times, this way of categorizing plants takes into account distinctions that European botanists miss. The Plateau people, for example, distinguished between two types of wild parsley on the basis of taste. The botanists, classifying the genus *Lomatium* on the basis of its physical characteristics, had put both into one species. Many Europeans noticed that native people were excellent botanists. James Mooney noted,

The Cherokee are close observers, and some of their plant names are peculiarly apt. The mistletoe, which never grows alone, but is found always with its roots fixed in the back of some supporting tree or shrub from which it draws its sustenance, is called by a name which signifies "it is married," or uda'li.

In addition to such descriptive names, native people also gave some plants sacred or symbolic names, which might only be used by priests or doctors. Among the Cherokee, corn was familiarly called Selu, or Corn Mother, the name of the woman from whose blood corn originated after her sons killed her. It also had another name the priests used—Awawe'la, "The Old Woman." This also referred to Selu.

Europeans found themselves at times depending upon the Indians' knowledge of plants for their survival. David Douglas was nearly starving during one of his forays into the Plateau region near present-day Spokane when at last he found the home of a pioneer named Finlay. Douglas reported that Mr. Finlay

> received me most kindly, regretting at the same time that he had not a morsel of food to offer me, he and his family having been subsisting for at least six weeks on the roots of a plant called by the natives all over the country, Camass, on those of Lewisia rediviva and on a black lichen which grows on the pines.

Lewisia rediviva is bitterroot; it was discovered by Meriwether Lewis on the westward journey and was reported to be a food plant. Black lichen grows on ponderosa pine trees and is strictly a starvation food. The fact that the Finlays were eating it shows how close to starvation they had come. Douglas also noted in his journal:

> Among the most interesting plants which I have just gathered is one of a genus perfectly distinct from Lilium, as its style is invariably three-cleft. It is abundant in light dry soil everywhere above the Falls [near the

junction of the Spokane and Columbia rivers]. I shall try to preserve its bulbs, as it is highly ornamental. The natives eat the roots, both raw and roasted in the embers, and collect in July a large store of them, which they dry in the sun and lay by for winter use.

The plant might have been either bitterroot or camas; Douglas doesn't say. Sometimes the native people taught the botanists a thing or two about their plants. The Crow cultivated *Nicotiana multivalvis*, and insisted that their tobacco was different from that of the Hidatsa. Eventually the botanists had to agree. The Hidatsa grew *N. quadrivalvis*. A Karok Indian described the differences between cultivated ("people's") tobacco and wild tobacco:

> Tobacco flowers are long necked, they are long flowers. The tobacco flowers are like somebody looking at you. The tobacco has pretty flowers, white ones. They are strong smelling ones. The people's tobacco flowers are not as white as the river tobacco flowers. The people's tobacco flowers are not very white.

⸙ THE SACRED COLORS ⸙

Indian corn comes in several different colors, each of which corresponded with one of the sacred directions. For some tribes, there are four directions: north, south, east, and west. Others have six; in addition to the four, they have up (above) and down (below). Five colors of Zuni corn correspond to east (white), west (blue), south (red), above (speckled), and below (black). Yellow corn has no special significance. The Tewa (who live in New Mexico) have six colored varieties of corn: blue (north), yellow (west), red (south), white (east), many-colored (above), and black (below). Nearly every tribe has a similar system by which the colors of corn are associated with the cardinal directions. The Hopis correlate white with east, blue or green with west, yellow with north, red with south, black with above, gray with the below. Some people make even finer distinctions. The Zuni distinguish between two shades of white corn; the shiny corn is used for hominy, but the duller white is sacred and is used for ceremonials. But even though some varieties of corn were more sacred than others, all vegetables were cared for equally throughout the garden year.

🌲 PREPARING THE SOIL 🌲

Indian gardeners generally did not use manure, or rotate crops to replenish the soil, so the first thing they did before planting seeds was determine whether the plot would sustain a good crop for another year. If so, they proceeded to clean up after the winter's storms. If not, in most areas they moved the gardens, or sometimes the whole town, in search of fertile soil. Plains tribes such as the Omaha and the Osage, who lived in a winter camp for the winter bison hunt and in a summer camp for the summer hunt and for the gardens, might shift the location of the summer encampment, or move the garden. Along the Missouri bottomlands, the Mandan and Hidatsa moved gardens to new locations while their towns stayed put. This meant that the gardens were often quite a distance away from the gardener. The Pawnee sometimes had to locate their gardens as much as eight miles from the village. The more settled people of the eastern woodlands, the Creeks, the Cherokee, or the Iroquois, who lived in the same towns all year round for several years, moved the towns every six to twelve years. When William Bartram asked why the Lower Creeks, who lived on the Chatahoochee (Chata Uche) river were breaking up their towns and moving, they told him that they needed fresh land for their plantations, and a new and more extensive hunting ground. Bartram observed that moving the town often brought these Creeks "into contention" with their neighbors.

Since fertilizers of any sort were seldom, if ever, used, people who gardened along rivers such as the Missouri or the Lower Colorado depended on the rivers to replenish the nutrients in the soil during annual flood cycles. The Missouri replenished the soil nutrients approximately every three years. The Lower Colorado gardens could be replanted about every year, partly because the new silt was rich in nutrients and partly because gardeners didn't necessarily plant in the same locations each time. The Cocopa and the Mohave moved to high ground during the floods; when the flood waters receded in the spring they planted their gardens in new soil. The people fed themselves in this way for hundreds of years until upriver dams and European farming disrupted the natural flood cycle.

Some people used other means to prolong soil fertility. The tobacco-growing Karok burned oak logs the season before they wished to plant, then sowed their seeds in the ashes, which were rich with added nutrients: magnesium, calcium, potash, and phosphorus. Burning also lowered soil acidity, and promoted the activity of nitrogen-forming bacteria. The Seneca, Onondaga, and other tribes of the Iroquois League planted beans among the corn hills. They knew nothing about the nitrogen cycle, or that the roots of the bean plants fix nitrogen, as do all legumes. They did know, however, that the corn plants thrived on this practice. For people who lived in the great forests, such as the Chippewa (northeast of Lake Superior), preparing the soil meant clearing a small space in the undergrowth where they could plant seeds. Woodland people in both the north (such as the Iroquois and the Algonquins) and the south (Creeks and the Choctaws) cleared whole plots by girdling trees and stripping a wide band of bark all around the tree. After the trees died, they burned the larger debris—branches and logs—and hauled out smaller branches and brush. Some people dug out stumps; others planted around them. The Algonquins did not use the ashes, as the Karok did, but carefully cleared both ashes and any weeds away from the garden plants.

After harvest in autumn, the Hidatsa and Mandan let horses into the gardens to browse on corn stalks, bean vines, and squash leaves. As soon as the big birds began their annual migration the following spring, the gardeners cleaned the ground of accumulated debris. To the surprise of early travelers, they also cleaned up the manure. They knew that manure contained weed seeds that often germinated, and to save themselves extra weeding they thoroughly cleaned the ground before planting. Traditional Indian gardeners did not usually believe in adding manure to the soil; besides not wanting to make more weeding work for themselves, they believed it to be unclean.

Early European observers noted that for the most part tilling the soil was an uncommon practice among Indian gardeners. There were good practical and spiritual reasons for not tilling the soil. Many people felt ill at ease when disturbing Mother Earth very much. Those who did dig into the earth often had a spiritual visitor show them how to plant. Selu visited the Cherokee and told her sons what to do. These gardeners and others felt tilling was unnecessary labor, when there was already so much labor in growing enough food for everyone's needs. Where soil moisture was precious, tilling would have dried out the soil with no benefit to the garden from loosening it. The Iroquois, the Delaware (who lived along the present Delaware River), the Choctaw, and the Algonquin, on the other hand, regularly tilled the soil every spring in preparation for planting. Other people, such as the Hidatsa and Mandan, simply raked up litter—uneaten cornstalks, manure, and other debris. They (and other people) fashioned rakes from deer antlers and willow shoots.

🌲 PLANTING TIME 🌲

Both corn and tobacco were planted, with appropriate rituals to ensure a good harvest. Every task, from placing the seed to singing the correct songs, had to be done properly if people were to eat well—or at all—during the rest of the year. In traditional Zuni methods of planting, the gardener used a long digging stick (approximately three-and-a-half feet long or longer, and one-and-a-half inches in diameter) with a short branch near the sharp end. Pushing this end into the soil with his foot, he made four deep holes to represent four of the cardinal directions. These he dug equally distant from the middle space, in this prescribed order: north, west, south, and east. To the left of the north hole he dug another to represent above. To the right side of the south hole he dug the hole for lower. As he planted he sang a song similar to this:

Off over yonder,
Toward the North-land,
Will it prove that my yellow corn grains
Shall grow and bear fruit, asking which I now sing.

In 1880, the Onondaga corn-planting festival lasted seven days. During the festival, the leaders confessed their sins in order to cleanse the situation in which the new corn would grow.

For the Osage, planting was a sacred act, conducted with appropriate rituals. Only women could plant, because the secret of giving life belonged to females. They planted in April, which as a result became known as a female month. The planting ritual required considerable agility on the part of the planters: first they scraped little hills together, then poked a hole in the sunny side of each one. Into each hole the woman dropped four to seven kernels, then covered the hole with one foot while singing sacred songs, keeping the rhythm with her digging stick, and looking at the sky. The Osage planting songs envisioned the crops to come, the seed sprouting, the stalk pushing through the soil, the silk appearing, the ears ripening, the harvest joy, and the happy homes with plenty to eat in the winter. As the Omaha planted, they sang a song to honor the corn plant. It envisioned healthy corn plants at all stages of growth from seed to harvest:

We sing the roots growing
We sing it clings to the earth

The people dance and sing sacred songs as they prepare to begin planting.

The people plant the tobacco seed.

LEFT
*Display of
Indian corn at
a Navajo fair
in Puerticito,
New Mexico,
in 1932.*

RIGHT
*Field of Indian
corn planted in
bunches. The
men are broad-
casting bait
against grass-
hoppers. A
Navajo reser-
vation, 1934.*

LEFT
*The man in
the foreground
shows how
deep this
cache pit is.
A Navajo
reservation,
1932.*

We sing it shoots from the ground
We sing it springs from joint to joint
We sing it sends forth the ear
We sing it puts a cover on the head
We sing it puts on a feather ornament
We sing it invites us to feel it
We sing it invites us to open it
We sing it invites us to see its fruit
We sing it invites us to taste its fruit
We sing it is good.

Bartram described how the Creek people went about planting. When the garden overseer had determined that planting should begin, he summoned the entire town by blowing on a conch shell. Everyone, carrying their garden tools, met at the village square and walked together to their gardens. Although each family had its own separate piece of ground, they began where the overseer told them, and covered the entire field. Gardening among the Creeks appears to have been a mixture of individual ownership and collective labor.

Not everyone, of course, had a prescribed planting ritual, but many tribes mistrusted plants whose seed was not sown according to ritual usage. Sunflowers, for example, self-sow readily wherever the wind carries the seeds, but the Mandan and Hidatsa people never harvested these plants because they thought wild sunflowers were not so good as those that had been properly sown and taken care of.

Aside from the rituals, planting techniques among the various cultures differed only slightly. Usually, these differences were caused by the environment rather than cultural or religious customs. People everywhere used digging sticks and their hands to make holes for seeds. Differences in methods of planting corn had more to do with available water than with religious attitudes or customs. Where people could depend on the water supply, as in the woodlands east of the Mississippi river, they dug shallow holes for corn seeds, then mounded up the soil around the growing stalks to support the plants. But in the arid West, particularly in the desert Southwest and the Great Basin, people dug holes perhaps six inches to a foot or more to reach damp soil under the dry surface. The Western Apache followed the custom of nearly all desert gardeners in using a digging stick to make the hole, then scraping out the dry soil with their hands until they reached moist soil. They then made a smaller hole in the moist soil and put in the seeds. As the seedlings grew and the soil dried, they watered and filled in the holes. When the level of the holes reached the surface, they mounded up the dirt around the stalk to support the plants against the constant strong winds.

For the Apache, the planting ritual mandated placing the seed in the order of the directions. They began in the east and continued up and down the garden, working their way westward until they were finished. Occasionally, they put seeds first in the hole at the center of the field, then planted to the east, south, west, and north until the field was done. They prayed and sang sacred songs as they planted corn, asking for a bountiful crop so the people would not starve. For other crops such as beans or squash, however, they had no rituals or prayers, for these plants were not sacred. Anyone could plant, but usually the owner of the garden asked a shaman or someone who knew the planting songs and rituals to place the seed. No menstruating or pregnant women could participate in planting, nor could anyone who had been struck by lightning or bitten by a snake.

Hopi gardeners, who were usually men, made holes with digging sticks about four paces apart and planted a cluster of seeds in each hole. When the plants came up, the gardener pulled up the weaker ones and left three or four of the stronger ones to mature. Some desert gardeners had observed that smoke slowed the evaporation of soil dampness, so they set out smudges among the corn hills to help retain moisture.

Seneca women gardeners soaked their seeds in water first, then gently placed them in the hills so as not to break the germs that had nearly burst through. For them, seven was a sacred number, so they sowed squash and bean seeds in every seventh hill.

⸙ WEEDING AND CULTIVATING ⸙

There was considerable variation among the tribes as to what constituted enough care. The more settled gardening people spent more time weeding and tending their gardens than did some of the buffalo hunters. In the desert, among the Navajo or on the Lower Colorado, it does not appear to have been the custom to thin young corn plants, for gardeners had an equal regard for all of them. In the Algonquin villages of the northeastern woodlands, as seventeenth-century engravings seem to indicate, gardeners staggered crops so as to harvest them at intervals. At the same time, one plot might have corn seedlings, another green corn, and a third ripe corn. There was, consequently, much to do—a woman might be tending seedlings, picking green corn, and harvesting ripe corn in the same week. Omaha gardeners hoed their gardens twice, once when the corn had sprouted, and again when it had grown about a foot. Up to this time, the mounds were carefully weeded by hand and the earth was kept free and loose. The mounds containing the squash, and those in which the melons were planted, were weeded and cared for until the second hoeing of the corn. After the second hoeing, the vegetables were left to grow and ripen without any more care while the people packed up and went on the summer buffalo hunt. They returned in time for harvest, when they hoped to find abundant crops. The Hidatsa also weeded by hand and hoed twice before the buffalo hunt, even though they did not abandon their villages or their gardens to hunt, as the Omaha did.

Straight rows and orderly beds were not important to native gardeners. Rather than laying out gardens along guided straight lines, those who planted in rows at all simply eyeballed them. Late in the nineteenth century, an anthropologist noticed that the Apache planted in regular rows, with even spacing between holes, although the rows were unmarked. Where they met an obstacle such as a tree or large stone, they continued the row beyond it rather than circling it or removing it. Likewise, some gardeners were not particularly concerned about weeding the garden simply for the sake of appearance. As long as the weeds did not deprive the food plants of precious water or choke them out, many considered weeding unnecessary.

Where weeding *was* necessary, some gardeners practiced intercropping, the technique of planting squash or pumpkins in the same plots with corn and beans. The big leaves of the squash and pumpkin vines shaded the ground and kept weeds out. Many Zuni gardeners kept the bottoms of the waffles free of weeds, but the ridges might have weeds growing on them. The weeds' roots helped keep the ridges intact when the waffles were flooded. Other Zuni gardeners preferred to keep everything weed-free. William Bartram wrote that the Creeks kept their extensive plantations of corn well cultivated and clean of weeds. By May their corn was well along, about eighteen inches in height. The beans, which they had planted on the cornhills, were also well sprouted.

On the Lower Colorado, the Mohave, Cocopa, and Maricopa people cultivated their gardens by hoeing their corn around the hills to break up the soil (and kill new weeds) in order for the young plants to emerge more easily. Larger weeds they pulled by hand. Often, gardeners hoed their crops just twice. On the lower Colorado, corn was hoed for the first time when both it and the tepary beans were eight inches tall. The corn was hoed a second time when it was about knee high, and the beans when they began to vine. While the gardeners were at it, they mounded up more soil around plants, especially the corn, to protect them from being blown by heavy winds. Between hills they did not hoe, but they did pull out the larger weeds. Less hoeing meant keeping the soil surface intact, which slowed evaporation of soil moisture.

⚶ CULTIVATING TOBACCO ⚶

The Karok cared particularly for their tobacco gardens. They fertilized them, sowed the seed, and weeded, although they did not cultivate the soil. At the proper time, they harvested the leaves, then cured, stored, and sold them in the extensive and widespread trade that existed among indigenous people of the West Coast. The Yuma and Mohave grew tobacco in secret, as a sidelight to their other gardening. In giving the seed to the meanest shaman of the tribe to plant, they sought to make sure it would be very bitter. Among other planting instructions was the requirement that it be planted during the hottest part of the summer, and at noon. After the seed was in the ground, no one but the planter was allowed to go near the garden until the tobacco was harvested. (Interestingly, despite all this care the Mohave smoked it rarely. There seems to have been a feeling that too much smoking winded people, and since they traveled hundreds of miles on trading expeditions, they needed a great deal of endurance.)

The Mohave method of cultivating tobacco resembled Zuni waffle gardening. First, they made a kind of basin around which a ridge of soil was scraped. Next, they loosened the soil inside, and poured in water carried by hand in gourds called ollas. When the water had drained through the soil, they dropped three or four seeds together a few inches apart. This method prevented the seedlings from growing up too thickly, because the shamans never thinned or transplanted them. They seemed to have weeded the garden throughout the growing season, and carried enough water to prevent the crop from drying out. When the tobacco was ready to harvest, they picked the leaves carefully and allowed them to dry for three or four days. Every so often, they taste-tested the leaves to determine if they had cured to the proper strength. When the leaves were ready, the shamans ground them up and stored them in a sealed olla to prevent pests from getting in.

Among the Crow, tobacco gardening was attended with elaborate ceremonies that were the province of a secret Tobacco Society. Planting time was determined by a Mixer, who had charge of mixing tobacco seeds with water and other ingredients and who determined (through means of a vision) the site of the garden. If no vision occurred, the members of the society used their best judgment as to where to place the garden. Each family belonging to the tobacco society had its tobacco plot, allotted by the society leader, which was set off with sticks marked according to the owners' visions. They built tiny sweat houses for the spirit of tobacco, to make it grow. The leader sang four songs, then poked a hole two inches deep. So the planting began.

Planting was accompanied by songs and dances in which the entire community participated. Between planting and harvest, certain rules were followed: pipes were smoked up and out until seeds were gathered, the members of the society abstained from certain kinds of foods, no grass was burned, and the songs sung by the community were only about tobacco, not weasels or otters. When a Mixer determined that the time was right, he combined the seed with water and manure and several other types of seed. Accompanied by appropriate songs and prayers to invoke the spirits to help the tobacco grow, this lasted most of a day. At the end, the seed was poured into the stomach of a cow bison. On the second day, the entire village dressed in their best clothes and, led by an esteemed woman, a keeper of a medicine bag, set out for the location of the garden. After marching a little way, the woman put a stick into the ground and hung the medicine bag on it. The musicians sang and drummed four songs (the sacred number), and everyone danced. Then they moved on to another place, and repeated the ritual with four more songs. This they did four times. After the fourth repetition, there was a horse race to the garden site. The winner would have good luck in the coming year. After planting, the society members slept at the garden to obtain another vision. At intervals they inspected the gardens, with songs and rejoicing at the progress of the plants. At the fourth inspection, they weeded the garden and wafted over it an incense made of wild carrots.

✣ HARVESTING THE CROPS ✣

The gardeners of each tribe worked hard at bringing their crops to harvest according to their view of the spirits' role and the amount of work their own role entailed. Many of the ceremonial observances throughout the year were held for one purpose—to ensure a good harvest. A good harvest meant enough food for the family, and (in some cultures) for the poor, for trade, and for visitors. With corn at the hub of their cultures, some people, such as the Iroquois or the Zuni, considered the harvest more important than the hunt, and the work of ensuring a good harvest began with religious observations around the time of the winter solstice. For the Iroquois, these ceremonies are the Midwinter Ceremonies; for the Zuni, the Shalako. When the milk rose in the new corn, the Creek people harvested their gardens and held the Feast of the Busk to celebrate the green corn. After that, they waited until it was fully ripe to harvest it. As with the planting, the whole town was called together to harvest the gardens. When they had finished, everyone put some of the crop into a central storage crib, the public granary. Contributions were voluntary, and each family put in as much as they wanted to or felt obligated to contribute. After it was filled, everyone was allotted enough to feed the family. This part they stored in their own granaries. If they ran short before the next harvest, they could help themselves from the public granary, which was also used to feed the poor, help other towns, feed travelers, and provision warriors and hunters. If everyone did his or her part correctly—spiritually and physically—throughout the year, people would eat. If the rains didn't come, though, or if grasshoppers ate the plants, something had gone wrong and the people were hungry until the next harvest.

Some of the harvested green corn was eaten immediately, a practice that struck some early observers as improvident. But sometimes the native people had been hungry for months, and the ripening of the corn meant that they could finally eat well again. Sometimes, harvests were very good, indeed. Observers reported that the Sauk and the Fox raised an estimated seven to eight thousand bushels of corn. Perhaps a thousand bushels of corn were sold to the traders and others. Each family kept about five bushels to take along and eat on the fall hunt. The rest they cached in pits to eat in the spring and summer, before the next harvest. The Huron might harvest a two- to four-year surplus of corn, beans, squash, sunflowers, and tobacco. This surplus both protected them against famine if crops should fail, and gave them an adequate supply for trade. Their yield, too, was often surprisingly good. The Huron annual harvest has been estimated at about 290,000 bushels on nearly 23,300 acres. The average yield was almost seventeen bushels per acre. Although many people commonly ate half the crop as green corn, a Mohave family might have roughly four baskets of unshelled corn to store for winter. (These baskets were about four feet in diameter, and three feet tall.) If the corn ran out, they subsisted on the seeds of grasses and other edible plants that they had stored during the summer.

Storing the Crops

Green Corn festivals, with their large feasts, celebrated the end of hunger. Yet no matter how hungry they might be, people were careful to store enough for later, in case future harvests should fail.

Corn could be shelled for storage or braided and hung to dry—sometimes in the houses, sometimes outside from scaffolds. Where the different corn colors had significance, special care was taken to store each color separately, to avoid crossing them. The

Iroquois, like the Hopi or the Navajo, braided some of their corn by turning the husks back and working them into a string. These they hung from the rafters or ridge poles in their houses, or in the longhouses. This corn dried on the ear, and when it was needed a woman would break off the ears, shell the corn, and cook it. Much of the corn, like beans, was shelled and dried, then stored in containers. The Iroquois used barrels made of bark, and either stored the natural kernels or parched them prior to putting them away. Within their longhouses were storerooms for barrels and other containers of provisions. A Frenchman named Sagard, who spent a year among the Huron (1523–1524), said the rows of braided corn hung like tapestry the whole length of the cabin. The people he observed stored enough for three or four years, and always tried to keep a plentiful surplus of corn for trade or emergency. Should one of the Six Nations have bad luck with their crops, the others would respond to the need, for a consideration or gratuitously, depending on the particular case and how friendly the others were with the needy people.

The Hopi dried their corn, beans, squash, and other vegetables by hanging them in the dry desert air. After it was dry, they stored it in large underground storehouses, or in their kivas, which were also underground. They hung the braids of corn and strings of squash from the rafters, and stored shelled corn and beans in pottery jars. The painter George Catlin visited the Mandan villages in the 1830s. The Mandans lived in earth lodges perhaps sixty feet in diameter. At the entrance, in front of the door, they built porticoes that served both as protection from sun or snow and as a drying rack for vegetables. Mandan gardeners cut squashes into thin slices, strung them on ropes made of grass, and hung them from corn scaffolds to dry. Shelled corn and beans they laid on the scaffolds, and braided corn was hung from the poles. If rain threatened, the people would cover the drying vegetables with tightly woven mats. After the produce had dried sufficiently, these people, like other Plains gardeners, stored it in cache pits. These pits were deep holes, almost cellars, dug sometimes in the floor of an earth lodge, sometimes between lodges. They were round, with an opening just big enough for a person to climb into, and lined with dried grasses and hides to keep ground water out. Before the gardeners left on the winter bison hunt, they sorted out an amount of vegetables to last the winter. Then they filled the cache with everything they did not need on the hunt, such as the rest of the harvest and extraneous household goods and valuables. These they laid down in alternate layers of corn, beans, squash, and other foods, with dried grass or rush matting between each layer. Each layer was packed down as tightly as possible. After the cache was nearly filled, they laid a thick layer of dried grass and matting on top, covered it with a hide, then filled that in with dirt. The dirt was tamped down hard, raked over with brush, or even walked upon by the villages' horses—anything to hide the cache from enemies. Disasters were always a possibility, however. Water could seep in and rot the stored food. Or, if they were not dug deeply enough, wolves or human predators would find them and dig them up.

Desert people practiced various forms of storage suited to their environment. On the Lower Colorado, severe flooding prevented the Mohave, Yuma, and Cocopa from constructing very extensive storage facilities. They simply filled storage baskets with corn, tepary beans, and mesquite beans, and placed them on platforms raised four to six feet above the ground. During high water, they grabbed the baskets and moved to temporary quarters on the bluffs above. On the Gila River, the Pima shelled the corn and beans and packed them in ollas. These they stoppered with clay and buried in the sand. Maricopa dwellings typically had an adjacent storehouse. The Cherokee, in common with many southern tribes, used a method of storage suited to the warm and humid south. In 1700, a traveler described it this way:

> They make themselves cribs after a very curious manner, wherein they
> secure their corn from vermin, which are more frequent in these warm

climates than in countries more distant from the sun. These retty fabrics are…well daubed within and without upon laths, with loam or clay, which makes them tight and fit to keep out the smallest insect, there being a small door at the gable end, which is made of the same composition and to be removed at pleasure, being no bigger than that a slender man may creep in at, cementing the door up with the same earth when they take the corn out of the crib and are going from home, always finding their granaries in the same posture they left them—theft to each other being altogether unpracticed.

People put shelled corn, beans, and dried squashes into bags and stored the bags in these wattle-and-daub containers. When they needed food, a slender adult or a child could crawl into the container and take what was needed. Afterward, they sealed up the door again.

🌲 WHAT DID THE GARDENS LOOK LIKE? 🌲

Unlike Asian or European cultures, American Indian cultures did not develop a specific garden aesthetic. This does not mean that their gardens were not beautiful, merely that their beauty might be difficult for Europeans to see. European aesthetics separates beauty from the beautiful object—form and function are distinct. In the Indian view, the beauty of an object could not be separated from its function. The beauty of a pot arose in part from its usefulness in holding water. So it was with gardens. The function of a vegetable garden was to produce food for the people's physical survival. The function of a tobacco garden was to produce tobacco for ceremonies and for gifts to the spirits. The function of either was itself beautiful, which made a garden beautiful, although the appearance of a tobacco garden hidden among forest undergrowth might not have seemed so to Europeans.

British, French, German, and Spanish immigrants to these

shores came from cultures with developed philosophies of land-scape art. English landscape design in particular was based on an ideal of nature expressed in geometric shapes, the same concept that had given rise to Palladian architecture. Not only that, but the English language, up to the late seventeenth century, did not include the concept of trees, forests, plains, mountains, and rivers—the natural world—among its definitions of the word "nature." To European eyes, native gardens did not have the orderly appearance associated with good gardening. The sizes of gardens were ambiguous; the spacing of plants was irregular; and garden shapes were, in modern terms, free-form. Flower gardening had no vogue until the nineteenth century, except in the gardens of the poor and the uneducated—a situation commemorated in the modern term "cottage garden." Furthermore, among the upper classes, the veg-etable or kitchen garden was relegated to the back of the house and screened so it would not be visible. Europeans thus had no background for appreciating native gardens. Yet Indian gardens could certainly be visually beautiful. For one thing, the plants themselves were beautiful—individually or in combination with other plants.

Indian corn plants were (and are) much smaller than modern hybrids. The plants stand between three and six feet, are usually about four feet high, and the cobs are usually four to six inches long. It's a very pretty plant, with graceful leaves that arch like the fronds of a fern. The flowers of the scarlet runner bean are a bril-liant carmine red, and somewhat resemble tiny irises. Some native sunflowers are not the giants we associate with the modern vari-eties. *Helianthus maximilianii*, for example, native to the Southwest, grows not much taller than the corn plants, with round, yellow flowers three inches wide. The corn plants' bright green leaves and tassels of silks, the yellow sunflowers, and the red bean flowers together would have made a dazzling combination. Buffalo Bird Woman, the Hidatsa gardener who described her gardens to Gilbert Wilson in 1917, told how she often planted sunflowers at the perimeter of her garden because they looked good there and gave passersby something pretty to see.

The Seneca and other Iroquois people combined beans and corn in the same hills. This practice probably resulted from a combination of mythic instructions and collective gardening experience. People did it because they knew it made better corn and beans, although they could not articulate the reasons in the scientific terms we use today. As the corn plants grew, they supported the bean vines and became entwined with the red flowers of scarlet runner beans. This combination was a friendly one, as the two Sisters embraced each other, while the third Sister (squash) spread its wide lobed leaves and white flowers along the ground. When the beans and squash flowered, and sunflowers bloomed, native vegetable gardens were a mass of red, yellow, and white flowers amidst the shiny, bright green curves of the young corn leaves. Tobacco gardens could be beautiful, too. The flowers of the various *Nicotiana* species are white, cerise, and purple. Their long, tubular flowers flare at the end, the better to accommodate the hummingbird's bill during pollination. In sunshine, especially with a breeze blowing, both kinds of gardens came alive with colors in motion, as hummingbirds and bees sought nectar.

All of this is not to say that distinctive garden styles did not exist among native people. Many people developed a particular garden style because of practical considerations, such as the need to provide enough water, or because traditional usage told them certain methods worked best, or because they had been instructed to do things a certain way in their myths. Zuni waffle gardens, for example, grew out of the necessity for conserving water. The Iroquois method of planting corn and beans in the same hills was a distinctive feature of their gardens, as wide, irregular spacing was characteristic of Lower Colorado desert gardens. Hidatsa gardens alternated a row of corn with a row of beans and a row of squash. Most Southwestern gardeners planted corn in clusters rather than each stalk by itself. The plants supported each other in the constant wind, and the groups have a shrubby appearance much different from the look of single stalks in straight rows found in Creek gardens. The Omaha gardened on small mounds, which helped to prevent the gardens from becoming waterlogged in heavy spring and summer rains. If rainfall were below normal, the raised mounds would keep the roots moist longer. These mounds were about eighteen by twenty-four inches, with flat tops, slanted toward the south for maximum exposure to the sun. Each mound was about two or three feet distant from the others and was planted with only one crop—corn, squash, and beans alternating.

The Pawnee were great gardeners who loved flowers. They valued the gallardia daisy or blanket flower *(Gallardia)* so much that they saved its seeds and planted them around their lodges, so they could enjoy the bright yellow and red daisylike flowers in summer. Some people picked the yellow flowers of the evening primrose *(Oenothera hookeri* or *O. missourensis)* for decorative bouquets. And when the redbud *(Cercis canadensis)* bloomed in late winter, they gathered it by the armful to cheer their homes with this sign of coming spring.

Another major factor in the appearance of a garden was the need to protect it. Some gardens were hidden. Tobacco gardeners such as the Blackfeet hid their gardens so that strangers would not discover the sacred plants and steal or destroy them. From time to time people would return to see how things were going, to assure themselves that undergrowth was not choking out the plants, or to do a little cultivating. Otherwise, the gardens grew by themselves. Regarding his meeting with the northwest coast tobacco gardener, David Douglas commented, "The natives do not cultivate [tobacco] near their camps or lodges, lest it should be taken for use before maturity. An open place in the wood is chosen where there is dead wood, which they burn, and sow the seed in the ashes." People also grouped their gardens together for security from enemies. This practice confused Europeans—sometimes the gardens looked like extensive fields and gave the mistaken impression that the gardens were larger than they actually were. Grouped together, Creek gardens covered so much ground that they appeared to be farms.

The Creek Confederacy and the Iroquois League were so powerful that they had no need to hide their gardens. Gardening together in the open gave them more than the usual measure of security in Indian America. (Even so, they periodically lost some of the crop to raiders.) Early European visitors to both Iroquois and Creek nations commented on how extensive the gardens were and how neat and tidy the fields looked, with the rows of corn plants stretching out through large, well-tended clearings in the forest. Although a village might have fifty acres or more under cultivation, the size of an individual garden was generally about an acre. Invading the Iroquois Genessee Valley in 1779, General Sullivan described the town of Genessee as "almost encircled with clear flat land extending a number of miles; over which extensive fields of corn were waving, together with every kind of vegetable that could be conceived." By the time he left, this beautiful smiling valley was a blackened ruin. General Sullivan's forces destroyed 100 acres of beans, cucumbers, watermelons, and pumpkins, and an estimated sixty thousand bushels of corn.

In the West, the Hidatsa and Mandan had rather small gardens, perhaps a quarter acre in size, more or less. The gardeners here were women. Among the Omaha, where men and women gardened together, gardens ranged from half an acre to two acres; occasionally, energetic gardeners might have three acres under cultivation—quite an undertaking before iron tools became common. On the other hand, those who gardened along the Lower Colorado or the Gila rivers, such as the Mohave, the Cocopa, or the Yuma, had fairly large gardens of an acre or even two. Here, however, the larger garden size was probably accounted for by how far apart the plants were spaced. Spacing, in turn, depended on the availability of water, although average annual rainfall (around ten inches) was about the same along the Missouri, Colorado, and Gila. The Missouri River never ceased to flow, even after the spring runoff from the Rocky Mountains had subsided. In contrast, after the Colorado and the Gila had subsided from their annual flooding, gardeners in those regions could not count on any more water for their gardens. They planted their seeds two feet apart or more, in order to give the roots room to find moisture. In general, the practice for determining spacing seems to have been to step off paces on the ground and put seeds in where it felt like a good place. This was not as haphazard as it sounds. Experienced gardeners develop a feel for their land, an understanding of what it will do, how plants will grow in certain places. Then, as now, a gardener may not be able to explain why he or she does it a certain way, but it works. Yields are good, and there is food for winter. In the desert Southwest, gardeners planted seeds wherever they found damp soil. The Apache planted corn anywhere from twenty inches to eight feet apart in their search for soil moisture.

The shapes of gardens depended on where they were planted. Those along streams followed the bends and curves of the ground's contours. Indeed, imposing rectangles on land is an invention of Europeans. The English gardening tradition, building on Platonic idealism, in particular admired geometry as the purest expression of ideal nature. Indian gardens might appear untidy. Sometimes weeds were allowed to grow where they did not interfere with the garden plants or rob them of water. Woodland gardeners such as the Ojibwa often contented themselves with clearing small spaces for individual garden plants among the undergrowth. The gardeners would make sure competition for water and nutrients didn't interfere with the garden plants. Some people marked off plots with fencing, less to show ownership than to keep out four-footed pests—deer, burros, or horses. The Creeks, however, did not originally fence their gardens, and Europeans' cattle were a terrible problem. Their white neighbors often simply let the cattle roam and forage for themselves. When protests did no good, native people shot the cows to protect their food supply.

❊ Life in the Garden ❊

Because people often located their gardens close together, the gardens were usually very social places. Gardening close to other people made gardening safer, and more fun, too. Mary Jemison, a white woman taken captive by the Iroquois in 1755, chose to remain with her adopted people, and lived with them for the rest of her life. In her eighties, long after she had forgotten how to write the English language, she described her life to a minister. For an Iroquois woman, she said, gardening was a social occupation. Women gardened together for safety and for the enjoyment of each other's company. They brought their children and looked after them. They had great fun joking, singing their personal garden songs, telling stories, and teasing each other. Afterwards, they went for a swim to wash the dust off, and clean up for the feast given by the owner of the garden. Each helper took home some corn soup, hominy, or bread. All in all, it would have been a rewarding day. Mary Jemison said,

> Our labor was not severe. Notwithstanding the Indian women have all the fuel and bread to procure, and the cooking to perform, their task is probably not harder than that of white women who have those articles provided for them; and their cares certainly not half as numerous, nor as great. In the summer season we planted, tended and harvested our corn, and generally had our children with us; but had no masters to oversee or drive us, so that we could work as leisurely as we pleased.

Iroquois women formed mutual aid societies such as the Good Rule society, which was made up of women who owned garden plots. The society's purpose was to help plan and carry out the work of gardening, and to provide for the elderly and infirm. The women nominated one older woman with leadership qualities as Corn Matron to oversee the gardens. She directed that certain gardens be worked when she decided they were ready. Several assistants reported to her on the gardens' progress, or she checked them herself. When she decided that a garden should be hoed, people would gather to help her work it. She would begin by placing her helpers in equal numbers on either side and a little behind her. Ahead of the others, she hoed to the end of the row, then stepped off the unhoed rows and took her place once more. Again, the others would take their places and hoe to the end, and repeat the procedure until the entire garden was hoed. Because of her diligence, the cultivation of the different gardens was kept even, and no garden received less care than another. Old women and those not strong enough for garden work helped out by babysitting. Gardening also provided an opportunity to educate the next generation in the ways of the tribe. Elder people passed on legends and corrected behavior. Even the smallest tots could place a seed in a hole and know they were helping to feed their people. This gave people a sense of being needed from an early age.

The Seneca also had a Society of Women Planters, and on the Plains, the Mandan and the Hidatsa formed the Goose Women Society, whose purpose was to benefit the people. It happened this way:

Long ago, at the time of beginnings, the people lived and gardened under the earth. The First Creator perceived that the world below was not as good as the world above, so he sent Good Fur Robe to guide the people upward. Good Fur Robe caused a bean vine to grow taller and taller until it was long enough for the people to climb all the way up. He told the people to bring their garden produce with them, for they would need to eat in the Upper World, and they began the long climb upward. Unfortunately, when most of them were on top, a very pregnant woman was too heavy for the vine and broke it, and so there are still some people who live under the earth. On top, Good Fur Robe became the first Corn Priest. He had traveled far to the south, to the island where lives the Old Woman Who Never Dies, with her assistants, the great birds that keep the food plants, each bird with its particular food. The Goose is the keeper of the corn, the Swan is the keeper of the squash, and the Duck is the keeper of the beans. Every spring, the Old Woman sends these birds north to signify that it is time to plant the gardens. She instructed Good Fur Robe in the duties of the Corn Priest and told him what he must to do to ensure a good crop. When he returned, Good Fur Robe organized the Goose Women Society into two companies and named their leaders. One company he told to paint their mouths black; the other company he told to paint their mouths blue. He named one woman as the Goose Woman, the chief of the whole society. It was her responsibility to look after the corn. To make the corn grow, Good Fur Robe said, she must bring him presents if there were an early frost in autumn so he could prevent damage to the crop. She would therefore have power to bring good to the people. And so it was. The people followed his instructions, and the crops were plenty and everyone had enough to eat. When Good Fur Robe knew that he would die, he named two men as his successors and instructed them to sing with the Goose Women. He drew a map of the world on buckskin, and carved a pipe of wood that only the Corn Priest was to smoke, for the red catlinite was the color of blood and not suitable. Then he named others to succeed the two, to be the Corn Priests after them. He instructed the men of the second group thus: "When we die, keep our skulls, and this map, and this pipe always with you. For as long as you have the map you shall know where you are on the earth, and as long as you keep our skulls you shall have our knowledge, and as long as you smoke this pipe our breath shall mingle with yours. Then the corn will always grow and the people shall have enough to eat."

The time before and during planting was filled with social events. The Goose Women entertained each other and their families with an exchange of feasts. They held the spring planting ceremony, with its dancing and singing and feasting. During planting the women talked happily across the fences separating each small plot, and sang songs to each other. It was a time of hope. After planting, however, gardening took on a lonely aspect. Hidatsa and Mandan women set up platforms in the gardens, where young, usually unmarried, women sat and watched for predators. Sometimes two girls would share a platform to watch two adjacent gardens. Young men might "happen by" when their favorite was on duty, for a little long-distance courting. Contact between unmarried boys and girls was strictly supervised in these tribes, so the young people would exchange songs instead of conversation. These songs were a good way for both to signal their intentions, and more than one young man went away discouraged or encouraged by the song a girl made up for him. Other garden songs reflect the discouragement every gardener knows. One of them, freely translated, goes something like this:

It is hard work
to care for a garden.
The blackbirds come
and eat it up.
Come, my brother,
and kill them.

Sometimes several Ojibwa families would garden together. In 1929, Nodinens, a seventy-four-year-old Ojibwa woman, described how her family had gardened during her childhood:

Each family had its own garden. We added to our garden every year, my father and brothers breaking the ground with old axes, bones, or anything that would cut and break up the ground. My father had wooden hoes that he made, and sometimes we used the shoulder blade of a large deer or a moose, holding it in the hand. We planted potatoes, corn, and pumpkins. These were the principal crops. After the garden was planted the Mide [medicine society] gathered together, made a feast and asked the Mide manido [chief deity] to bless the garden. They had a kind of ceremony and sang Mide songs. Old women could attend this feast, but no young people were allowed. Children were afraid when their parents told them to keep away from such a place. The gardens were never watered. A scarecrow made of straw was always put in a garden. In the spring we dug wild potatoes, ate pigeons boiled with potatoes and with meat. We went to get wild potatoes in the spring and a little later the blueberries, gooseberries, and June berries were ripe along the lake shore. The previous fall the women had tied green rice in long bundles and at this time they took it out, parched and pounded it, and we had that for food. Next came the rice season. The rice fields were quite a distance away and we went there and camped while we gathered rice. Then we returned to our summer camp and harvested our potatoes, corn, pumpkins, and squash, putting them in caches which were not far from the gardens.

3

THE
CEREMONIAL
YEAR

In the beginning of the world, the people had being but no form, and lived as nebulous breaths of air. Yearning to have forms, they cried out for help and Crow came to their aid. But when they had bodies, they needed food. A woman named Wakonda went out and found an odd thing: little mounds had erupted on the ground. A few days later, she went out again and saw that strange green plants had sprouted out of the mounds. What a very odd thing, indeed! She watched these grow tall, and ears of red corn soon sprouted from the stalks, which she took home to her husband and children. They roasted the ears in the fire and ate them and found them delicious. Because the corn came to them in this way from Wakonda, neither this man nor this woman nor their children nor any of their children's children partake of the red corn, for to them it is sacred.

And even after they became the Omaha, the people remembered. When the plum trees and the cherry trees were full of fruit, and when the small animals and insects were awake and out of their burrows, they knew it was the season for the ceremonial of the maize. Then the Sacred Pole was cut from a young cottonwood tree, or a willow tree that grew by the river, for it drew water unto itself and remembered when it stood before the Sacred Tent of the White Buffalo. And the reason it was done this way is this: Wakonda had given the people both the buffalo and the corn, and the white buffalo is also sacred, for some believe it is the spirit of Wakonda made manifest. This is why the mature cornstalk is painted on white buffalo hide with which the sacred tent is covered. For the corn and the buffalo together are the life of the people. When the pole had been cut and peeled, the sacred medicine bag (containing human hair) and four bunches of tobacco were tied to it and it was planted. Then the descendants of the original people, to whom the red corn was sacred and who had guarded it all year, gave ears of red corn to those whose duty it was to sing the ritual of the maize. When the ritual had been sung, the singers gave the sacred kernels to those whose duty it was to choose the date for planting the corn. These people gave four kernels to each family in the tribe as a sign it was time to plant the corn. In this way, the harvests would be plenty and the people would not go hungry.

⁂ THE SACRED PLANTS ⁂

In the traditional view of the gardening people, there were four sacred plants—corn, squash, beans, and tobacco. Of these, corn and tobacco were the most important. Corn was preeminent in the people's physical survival, and corn and tobacco together were central to their spiritual survival. Tobacco carried the people's prayers to the spirits, was a pleasing offering to them, and joined the breath of the people with the wind, which was the breath of the universe. Corn was both substance and spiritual entity, a gift of the spirits and a spirit itself. In the Hopi view, when corn was eaten its flesh became their flesh, so that when they offered corn meal to the spirits, they offered their own flesh. Being spirit as well, because it was divinely created, corn in many forms—corn-meal, corn pollen, cornhusk masks, or corn stalk—was also a spiritual offering. Gifts of sacred cornmeal during important cere-monies feed the spirits, soothe them, and make them happy with the people. A Zuni baby is given an ear of sacred white corn to carry throughout life. The Fox people called corn "tamina," and said it was a *manitou*, one of the mysterious cosmic powers inhabit-ing the earth. Wisaka, the primary manitou, created humans and then made corn for them. The people knew it was a manitou because after they ate it they felt stronger. They also felt capable of doing more than they could after eating any other food. Accord-ing to Pawnee belief, people were descended from the union of the Great Spirit and corn. They told George Bird Grinnell, "We are like seed and we worship through the corn." Unlike nearly all of the other gardening tribes, however, the Pawnee practiced ritual sacrifice of a human captive as part of their planting ceremony.

The Pima, like many people, believed that tobacco came from the gods. When it was smoked, it died and released its own spirit, which joined the spirits of the universe that influenced the fate of humans. In its ceremonial use, tobacco put a person in a state of mind to be in contact with the spirits. Its smoke lifted prayers to the deities, and joined the human spirit with the wind, which was the spiritual breath of the natural world. In their midwinter thanksgiving ceremonies, the Seneca sent their thanks via tobacco smoke wafting upward to the Maker of Life.

During one Navajo Yeibitchai curing ceremony held in 1880, the priests fed sacred corn pollen and hummingbird feathers to the spirits of mountains and rocks, and offered them precious stones and tobacco "lighted by the sun's rays." In exchange they asked for a "good dance," so that the person for whom the dance was held might be cured. Native people believed that illnesses were caused by being out of favor with the spirits, or in Navajo terms, being out of harmony with one's surroundings. Navajo curing ceremonies were held to bring the patient back into harmony, so that he or she could again "walk in beauty." Both tobacco and corn were used in these ceremonies (although not just by the Navajo) to enlist the help of the spirits in restoring the patient to physical and spiritual health. Tobacco in this sense was a medicine in that it operated on the spiritual plane to cure an ailment.

🌲 PLANES OF BEING 🌲

In the view of traditional gardening cultures, it was as if all life existed in a circle, with planes of being radiating outward from the spiritual core. Everything exists simultaneously in their material and in their spirit forms, but the sacred plants held a special place. Corn and tobacco, and sometimes squash and beans also, occupied simultaneously the outer plane as garden plants and the spiritual core (along with the bison in some Plains cultures). Among different cultures the plants inhabiting both circles may vary. For the Seneca and other Iroquois tribes, these were corn, beans, and squash—the Three Sisters. In the Navajo view, they were corn, beans, squash, and tobacco. The Karok, the Kutenai, the Blackfeet, and the Crow gave spiritual value only to tobacco.

In the illustration on the next page, the outermost plane contains the gardens, where corn, beans, squash, and tobacco, as well as other cultivated plants, exist as their material selves. They also exist in spiritual form in the inner plane, at the spiritual center of life. The people, who work the gardens, inhabit the second plane. Ceremonies occupy the third plane, between humans and the spirits in the fourth plane. People on their own spirit level invite the spirits to these ceremonies, where they interact with the spirits represented by cornhusk masks or kachinas and prevail upon them to intermediate with spirits of the plants on the people's behalf, to make them grow and be fruitful. The spirits, if properly treated and pleased with the people's gifts, will then intercede with the spirits of the plants and animals (innermost plane) on which the people's survival depends.

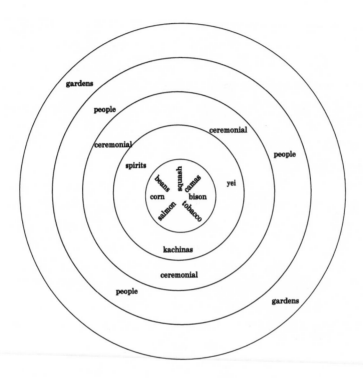

Everything in the world was held to have had a common spiritual origin. An Apache myth tells how a mountain spirit married the daughter of Raven Chief and took her to the underworld. From there, he sent back presents of corn and seeds with instructions on how to grow them. Gardening is integral to the legend of the origin of the Mandan and Hidatsa. Old Woman Who Never Dies was one of the original beings, not created by any other spirit, present with First Creator. She has a garden, and the blackbirds, who come from the red corn, are her helpers. She lives on an island in the South, and the spirits of vegetation, especially garden plants, go to her each year to spend the winter.

Medicine bundles are connectors of the human with the spirit world, and the contents of an Old Woman bundle at the beginning of this century included, among other things, a wooden pipe with a goose's head on the stem, which signified the beginning and ending of a garden season; some white sage for cleansing the body after working in the garden; a gourd rattle from one of the garden plants; and the head of a blackbird, because of the bird's habit of eating bugs harmful to the garden. A whistle made from the stalk of the sunflower, when blown in summer, brought rain; blown in winter it brought blizzards. An ear of yellow corn, a few beans, a small pumpkin, and some dried sunflowers might also be found in the bundle.

Sometimes there were similarities in beliefs among people living far apart. Old Woman Who Never Dies rejuvenated herself every spring, and sent the big birds north from her island to signify her return to life. She resembles the Navajo Changing Woman, who also ages as the year commences and renews herself in youth every spring. All of these beliefs assume a common spiritual origin both of the people themselves and of their sustenance. The common origin in spirit gave native people a sense of kinship, at least on the spirit plane, with other parts of creation. Despite this spiritual kinship, however, Indian people often had an ambivalent attitude toward other creatures. They were too important to be taken lightly, but they often could not be fully trusted. Coyote, for example, in many native cultures is both a hero and a trickster. Crow is another such creature. The Fox people believed that crows knew the secrets of healing the sick with medicinal herbs. But when the birds were caught stealing corn, people killed them. Among the Mandan, Hidatsa, and Ojibwa, the crow was thought to bring the vital spring rains. But in the Zuni story of how the crow became black, the crow proves himself to be unreliable.

Crow was at this time a handsome fellow, with white shoulder-bands and a blue back. The Corn Maidens had got lost, and the people were at their wits' end how to find them. Two warriors sought out the Crow, Old Heavy Nose, who was scratching in a rubbish heap to find a meal. When he heard their request, Crow said, "I'm much too hungry to go on a hunt like that, even if I could find them. You people pick the bones too clean." The warriors said, "We will feed you. Then you can look for them." "Now, you're talking," said Crow. They brought him into their house and offered him tobacco. He took such a great puff of smoke that it filled his feathers, and ever since, crows have been black all over. Spotting an ear of corn in a forgotten corner, Crow promptly stole it. As he flew away, the people heard him say, "This is the last you'll ever see of the maidens." But later he took pity on the people and tried to find them. To no avail. He reported back that although he had a sharp eye for their flesh, he could find no trace of them. Ever since, Crow has had such a fondness for corn that he will steal it whenever he can.

Whether or not they were gardeners, native people believed almost universally that life forms and phenomena had both material and spiritual existence, and that matter and spirit were not opposed. The material thing seen or heard is an outward representation of its inner, spiritual, reality. Further, because everything exists in body and spirit at once, it can be transformed from its existence on one plane into existence on the other plane. This transformation of the material into the spiritual and back again allowed people to directly communicate with spirits on their own level. For gardening people, ceremonies are a society's way of communicating with the spirits. During the ceremonies, the people who impersonate the spirits act on behalf of the people. The Zuni and the Hopi communicate with these spirits through deities called kachinas, who are impersonated by people with masks and costumes. The act of wearing the mask and the costume transforms the person into the kachina they are impersonating, while at the same time remaining themselves. The Crow kachina, for example, has human hands and feet, turquoise armbands, and a black, hoodlike mask with a large yellow beak and eyes outlined in turquoise. Through these kachinas, the people communicate with the spirits necessary to their survival.

The Seneca make cornhusk masks to stand for spiritual beings that can cure the sick and restore health and harmony. These beings share with humans their power to cure in exchange for gifts of tobacco and cornmeal. In Navajo religion, there are no kachinas and no supreme deity, but the *yei*, or minor deities, can be of great assistance. The legends tell how two of the yei, Talking God and House God (the latter is the god of growing things, particularly gardens), helped the Navajo acquire corn.

A man who wanted to learn songs convinced Talking God and House God to take him to where the songs were. Along with them traveled the Naaskiddi, whose hunchbacks are clouds that contain the seeds of all vegetation. The people in the land of songs gave the song-hunter many songs. They showed him dry paintings to go with the songs, and taught him how to mix the paints from various colors of sand. The song-hunter remained with them until the corn was ripe. The songs taught him how to eat corn, and he carried some of it back with him to the people, who had not seen corn before. In turn, he taught them how to raise it and how to eat it.

These yei appear in the Navajos' Night Chant and Mountain Chant. In both, corn and other cultivated plants are primary symbols—in the Night Chant, one of the four great sand paintings shows a corn plant at the center, which signifies that corn is the primary substance of life. These are curing ceremonies, whose most immediate purpose is medical: to cure a disease by restoring the patient to harmony with the world. The Mountain Chant is also used for invoking the unseen powers on behalf of the people at large for various purposes, particularly for good crops and abundant rains. During the last three or four days of the rituals, a large and complex sand painting was drawn on the floor of the medicine lodge each day and destroyed at the end of the ritual each night. Each one took about seven or eight hours to complete, and was of varying size, some as large as twenty by fifteen feet. A Navajo myth uses one of these sand paintings in its retelling:

A disobedient youth is captured by the Utes and is about to be whipped to death when he is rescued by the yei Qastce'elci. The yei leads him home, and during the journey the youth visits the yei's home. It is a house made of corn pollen, with a door made of daylight. The yei offers him hospitality and feeds him white corn meal and corn pollen. During a later part of the journey home, the youth is led to a den belonging to four bears who are lounging around a fire that burns with no wood. Instead, the flames rise from four pebbles: a black pebble in the east, blue in the south, yellow in the west, and white in the north. Each bear is colored to match the pebble nearest it. When the bears demand tobacco, the Navajo fills a pipe and lights it at the fire. But after taking only a few puffs, each bear passes out in turn. The boy revives them, and they give him a place at the east side of the fire. Although they offer him food from their stores of corn meal, the yei warns the boy not to eat. Then, from a corner of their cave they unroll a great sheet of cloud, on which are painted the forms of the yeis of the cultivated plants. This signifies that these garden plants—corn, beans, squash, and tobacco—were a gift to the people from the bears.

This painting from the bears' cave is surrounded by a rainbow, the Rainbow Girl, open to the east. In the center is a bowl of water surrounded by sunbeam rafts on which stand the four yeis of the sacred cultivated plants. They wear kilts of red sunlight decorated with sunbeams, and dangling earrings and bracelets made of turquoise and coral, the ancient Navajo jewels. Their legs and forearms are of black rain clouds with lightning, and they carry rattles. Each is colored the same as his corresponding sacred plant, which stands at his left hand. The corn plant and the eastern yei are white; the beanstalk and the southern yei are blue; the western yei and his pumpkin vine is yellow; the northern yei and his tobacco plant are black. Each of the four sacred plants grows from five white roots in the central waters. The painting illustrates how the cultivated plants correspond to the four cardinal directions that orient the people to the earth.

In the desert Southwest, rain is obviously a chancy thing for the gardeners. Desert people composed songs as prayers for rain. Usually, these songs imagined that something connected with rain was happening, as if it were actually occurring. The Pima had an entire cycle of rain songs. Because they lived away from most major rivers, Navajos also included prayers for rain in their ceremonies. This Navajo song describes hearing the thunder and grasshoppers that precede and follow a rain storm.

The voice that beautifies the land!
The voice above,
The voice of the thunder
Within the dark cloud
Again and again it sounds,
The voice that beautifies the land.

Mandan drying rack for corn.

LEFT
Digging stick with prong that was used for hard soil.

RIGHT
Rake made from a stick.

LEFT
Nodinens, an Ojibwa (Chippewa) woman who told Frances Densmore about her people's gardening traditions (see pages 56–57). She was seventy-four years old when this picture was taken.

RIGHT
Sacred tent of the Omaha. The white buffalo hide with corn stalks painted on it unites, symbolically, the people's two main sources of food.

The voice that beautifies the land!
The voice below;
The voice of the grasshopper
Among the plants
gain and again it sounds,
The voice that beautifies the land.

Another way of dealing with the lack of rain is to ask the kachinas to intercede, as the Zunis did in this instance:

By August in the high desert the summer rains were needed, for the crops had not come. The sun glared while temperatures soared beyond memory. Late in the afternoon of a day when heat waves had shimmered above the corn plants, clouds gradually obscured the sun. A sudden wind darted here and there around the houses and streets of Zuni, filling the air with sand. Into this sandstorm, a group of eleven kachinas emerged from behind a curtain covering a doorway. No kachina was like any other; one was gray with white symbols, one was white with green symbols, another had more red, this one had some blue. Bending slightly against the wind, they walked up a narrow passageway to a sandy courtyard hemmed on all sides by adobe houses. Except the kachinas, everything—even the air—was the tan color of sand. In the storm, they were a shifting kaleidoscope of white, green, gray, and bits of red. The drum boomed out its complex rhythm, and the sand swirled about them. They danced, and chanted solemn and unknown words as old as time. The gourds in their hands shook with a sound between a click and a shhh that echoed the shuffling of their feet in the sand. They danced to bring rain, to honor the gods, to ensure the people's survival.

In another Zuni story, water contains all the seed of the world, and from this *Yanauluha* (contained-seed-substance) comes everything else, especially corn. But even before corn, tobacco existed; it was to the Tobacco People and others that the seed of corn was given. The corn received its seven colors when leading priests planted the seed with reverent chanting and prayers, by the light of the great constellation now also called the Big Dipper. They planted variously colored prayer plumes around it—yellow on the north, blue on the west, red on the south, and white with the east. The last three they planted according to the handle of the constellation. In this way the colors of corn were divinely united with the cardinal directions and with the stars.

The gardening year naturally parceled itself out by the tasks that made the crops grow: soil preparation, planting, cultivation, and harvest. The ceremonial year supported the gardening year with ceremonies and rituals designed to enlist the help of the spirits in bringing about a successful crop that would ensure the people's survival for another year. Some ceremonies were not necessarily tied to gardening tasks but were held to enlist the spirits' help in organizing the forces of nature to ensure a successful harvest. For example, winter solstice festivals such as the Midwinter Ceremony of the Iroquois tribes, the Zuni Shalako, or the Hopi Wuwuchim, Soyal, and Powamu occurred when the year was at its darkest. These observances invoked spiritual aid by summoning the spirits and reenacting the origins of the tribe to remind everyone, spirit and human, of their interdependence. Among the Cherokee, the ceremonial year began in March, with the first new moon of spring. October brought the Ceremony of the Great Moon, followed later in the month, or in November, by the Celebration of Friendship. And nearly everyone celebrated spring, with its promise of plenty.

The people of the Iroquois League believed in three orders of spirits: those that focused on the earth, those that ruled above the earth, and those that controlled the universe. Traditionally, a different ceremony was held for the each type of spirit. These ceremonies were intended to bring people into harmony with a particular class of spirits. For example, the spiritual nature of the Three Sisters was celebrated in an elaborate round of thanksgiving festivals that lasted all year. The two major ones were the Midwinter Thanksgiving ceremony, celebrated about the time of the winter solstice, and the Green Corn ceremony, held in August. The Midwinter ceremony ushered in the New Year by asking for assistance during the coming year as well as giving thanks to the spirits for ensuring the people's survival during the previous year. No two ceremonies were exactly alike, but all followed a basic plan that allowed for considerable improvisation. The Onondaga, prior to their Green Corn festival, feasted, danced, and gambled for four days. Gambling was a religious act that tested their luck and their standing with the spirits. If the spirits favored a person, he or she won; if not, loss and poverty could be the result.

The Hopi ceremonial year began in the winter with three important ceremonies: Wuwuchim, then Soyal, and last, Powamu. These ceremonies reflected the three phases of creation. In November, Wuwuchim commemorated the first dawn of creation, with the germination of all earthly life forms—plant, animal, and human. During this ceremony, elders of the Tobacco clan and the Side Corn clan smoked ritually prepared pipes of tobacco and sang seven songs. The first three songs told how the world was prepared, life began, and vegetation appeared. The next four pertained to the cycle of the gardening year: corn was planted, corn grew, the people harvested corn, and the Creator sent rain for the corn. If the ceremonies were perfectly performed, the elders would know by the rainbows whether or not they would have a good harvest. The ceremony of Soyal took place during the winter solstice. Soyal celebrated the dawning of life, with rituals to ensure that corn grew. Special *pahos* (prayer sticks) were made to represent life yet to come. Seeds were blessed, and their origin from the mother of all life was remembered. A young girl was sacrificed—physically, in earlier times, but in later years symbolically by whispering her name to a special prayer stick (this was something like being hexed). In this way, the people remembered that death was part of life, that even in germinating, a seed gave up its own form to become the plant. Powamu, the Bean Ceremony, was the third of the great winter ceremonies. Powamu portrays the final phase of creation, the germination of the seeds. Much of the ceremony took place in the *kiva*, the underground chamber that commemorated the people's origin in the worlds below this, the fourth, world. In the first ritual of this ceremonial, beans were used because they germinated quickly, and the whole sprout could be eaten in subsequent rituals. After four days, when the seeds had sprouted, the Bean Dance was held. The Crow Mother kachina, in her black wedding finery, carried the sacred spruce, bean sprouts, and corn on a tray throughout the village.

In the spring, when planting was near, the women's societies began the rituals specifically relating to gardening. The purpose of one such ritual, Lakon, was to watch over the crops, particularly corn, in the fields. From planting till harvest, the Lakon participants tried to keep their thoughts in harmony with the meanings of the songs to guard against evil entering and ruining the crops. A second harvest ceremony, Marawu, occurred when corn began to dry at the edges and the melons were ready to pick. In addition to these ceremonies, people took care in planting and while the plants were growing to say the right prayers and to plant the pahos properly in order to enlist the aid of the spirits of the crops. In this difficult desert environment, every possible care was taken to bring about a successful harvest. Not until mid August, as the crops ripened and the shells of pumpkin and squash hardened, did any other major ceremonies take place. The Flute and the Snake-Antelope ceremonies occurred on alternate years. The Snake-Antelope ceremony, in particular, has gained fame from its use of live rattlesnakes during the Snake dance, but less well known to casual audiences is the ancient purpose of both these ceremonies—to ripen the crops and bring late summer rains to wash new soil into the gullies for a second planting of corn.

In the Pawnee calendar, the ceremonial year began with the first thunder in the spring. Soon after, at the right time, priests gave sacred seed corn to the people. This seed corn was believed to be a direct descendent of the corn that was given to the mother of the human race. It was this corn that provided the seed of the gardens in spring. Because the corn had come from a sacred source, it had to be taken care of properly and with the right observances, or it would not germinate. The harvest ceremony, which ended the ceremonial year, was followed by a rite known as "making Mother Corn." The ears of corn in all the sacred bundles were replaced from the freshly gathered harvest. Dancers dramatized certain acts of the gods, and the people made offerings and sacrifices. A group of men would capture a young girl, perhaps thirteen or fourteen, from an enemy tribe. They would treat her with deference and kindness until she was led out and sacrificed with an arrow through her heart. This practice was discontinued, so the story goes, early in the nineteenth century when a young man took pity on a captive girl. The night before the ceremony, he abducted her and took her to the nearest fort to be reunited with her relatives. He was a fighter of some renown who used his influence to stop the practice.

The Mandan Corn Priest was the keeper of sacred seed corn. In exchange for a gift, he gave some to each woman, who mixed it with her own corn to make her crop more productive. Another of his duties was to purify the seed before it was planted. He took the map of the world, handed down from the first Corn Priest, Good Fur Robe, and hung it in his lodge so that one edge touched the floor. Below it he placed the seed corn, and sang songs that only he had a right to sing. After ceremonially smoking and asking for the spirits' help, he brushed all over the seed with mint to cleanse it. Between the ceremony of purifying the corn and its harvest, the Corn Priest was considered sacred. During this time, he remained in his lodge, eating only dried vegetables and last year's corn. Every spring, after the big birds flew north, the Goose Women held their own ceremony. They began with a feast, and afterwards danced and sang. One song reflected the people's recognition of the goose:

A Mandan woman, a member of the Goose Women society who was working in her garden, was kidnapped one day by enemies raiding for corn. After many sorrowful weeks, she managed to escape. But as she trudged across the waterless prairie, she began to despair of ever reaching her home again. One day, she lay down and sent her spirit skyward, to die if she must. But her spirit encountered a goose in its flight, whom her spirit recognized as Mother. Eventually, she reached home to live with her people and sing this song in her garden, the song of recognition:

My youngest daughter,
Here you are.
Yes, Mother,
I am here.

The ceremonial year for the Creek confederacy ran from April to October, with the high point in August when the people held the Boskita, or Busk. This new-year festival lasted about a week, and coincided with the ripening of the corn. William Bartram described a Busk festival that he saw around 1776:

It was a time of cleansing and renewal. Everything was made new and clean to prepare them for the new year, and to welcome the new corn. People threw out old pots and pans, burned old clothes and bedding,

and swept out their houses. They cleaned the main square and all public buildings. They even brushed all leftover grains out of the granaries.
When every place had been cleaned, they gathered everything into a big
heap and burned it in the central square. Then they put out all the fires
in the town, and cleaned the hearths.

On Busk day, the fourth day of the festival, the people cleaned
themselves from inside out by drinking an emetic, the famous "black
drink," said to be made in part of snake root and tobacco. After purg-
ing themselves, they fasted for three days. During this period, the leaders
of each town proclaimed a general amnesty for criminals (except some
murderers) and allowed all exiles to come home. On the fourth day,
they brought the new year on by eating new food prepared from new
corn at new fires. The women harvested some of the new corn and
other first fruits from the orchards. They lighted a stick from the new
fire in the square, and took it home to kindle the new fires laid on their
hearths. Over these new fires, they prepared their best and most festive
recipes with the green corn, and brought the dishes to the central
square. There, everyone had gathered, now dressed in new clothes and
their best ornaments. They served the new food with a sense that everything was new again.

Like most people, the Cherokee watched anxiously for the
first ears of corn. They sought to control weather and growing
conditions by winning the spirits' favor with elaborate ceremonies
whose purpose was to ensure a good crop. The anthropologist
James Mooney described this ritual as he observed it before 1900:

After the last working of the crop, the priest and an assistant—generally the owner of the field—went into the field and built a small
inclosure [sic] in the center. Then entering it, they seated themselves
upon the ground, with heads bent down, and while the assistant kept

perfect silence the priest, with rattle in hand, sang songs of invocation to the spirit of the corn. Soon, according to the orthodox belief, a loud rustling would be heard outside, which they would know was caused by the Old Woman bringing the corn into the field, but neither must look up until the song was finished. This ceremony was repeated on four successive nights, after which no one entered the field for seven other nights, when the priest himself went in, and if all the sacred regulations had been properly observed, was rewarded by finding young ears upon the stalks. The corn ceremonies could be performed by the owner of the field himself, provided he was willing to pay a sufficient fee to the priest in order to learn the songs and ritual. Care was always taken to keep a clean trail from the field to the house, so that the corn might be encouraged to stay at home and not go wandering elsewhere.

To the Cherokee, the Green Corn ceremony was the most solemn occasion of the ceremonial year. It marked the end of hunger, for that time, and celebrated the survival of the people for another year. It took place as soon as the corn had ripened enough to eat; there was no set date for the observance because it depended on when the corn milk rose in the kernels. Usually, however, it took place early in August. One of the dances performed during this ceremony was the Groundhog Dance. It consisted of a line of dancers who advanced and retreated according to calls from a dance leader, and it had its basis in the legend of a groundhog who was caught by seven wolves.

As a groundhog was about to be killed and eaten by wolves, he said, "Wait a minute." The wolves, who don't appear to have been extremely intelligent, paused. The groundhog said, "When we find good food we must rejoice over it, as people do in the Green Corn dance. I'll lean up against seven trees in turn and you will dance out and then turn and come back, as I give the signal, and at the last turn you may kill me."

The wolves were very hungry but they wanted to learn the new dance, so they told him to go ahead. At each song the groundhog took another tree, and each tree was a little nearer to his hole under a stump. He began the seventh song and kept it up until the wolves were way out in front. Then he gave the signal, "Yu!" and made a jump for his hole. The wolves turned and were after him, but he reached the hole first and dived in. Just as he got inside, the foremost wolf caught him by the tail and gave it such a pull that it broke off, and the groundhog's tail has been short ever since.

The Tohono-O'odham people (formerly known as the Papago) celebrated harvest-time with the Vikita/Navitco ceremony. During this festival, the medicine men ritually sprinkled everyone with corn flour to help them stay healthy, then ritually cleansed themselves with a dusting of corn meal. During the event, the people of each village compose songs and speeches. A significant component of the festival, besides celebrating the harvest, was to encourage a good crop for the next year. This was done by composing songs that envisioned a happy outcome. The following song was recorded during a 1919 Vikita ceremony. Achi, Winyim, Akchin, and Anekam are names of villages. These names were repeated in the songs to bring a good harvest to each one.

> Over there the clouds in a row come out
> Over there our field above, there the corners
> There come out. It thunders, it rains.
>
> In Achi our field far off is heard to shake.
> Above shining clouds come out.
> Here our field, it rains, corn springs up.

Big house where it rains.
Up above clouds come out
We'll hear that thundering, it rains.

In Winyim our fields, in Winyim our fields,
On them corn springs up.
Achi our fields, Achi our fields
On them corn comes out
Akchin our fields, Akchin our fields
On them corn springs up.
Anekam our fields, Anekam our fields
On them corn springs up.

Achi our field on water ran ran
Here, look, people! Yonder clown ears of corn
Bears away, bears away!

All stick are there. All stick are there.
All we stand up and lay across.
All we stand up and lay across.

Dying world here lay
Dying world here lay
Above corn comes out.
Bend stalks.
Above comes out. Rains.

Little green Montezuma is coming out.
Little white corn is coming out.
Many clouds rain on me.
Many clouds rain on me.
Clouds come out, rain on me.

The Pima people, who were closely related to the Tohono O'odham, also celebrated the Vikita and had similar songs designed to bring rain. The song below was one of a cycle recorded by the anthropologist Frank Russell during a Vikita ceremony in 1904. It and its companion songs envision the crops standing in the fields.

Hi-ihiya naiho-o! let us begin our song.
Let us begin, rejoicing. Hitciya yahina-a.
Let us begin our song, let us begin, rejoicing.
Singing of the large corn. Hitciya yahina-a.
Singing of the small corn. Hitciya yahina-a.

Hi-ihiya naiho-o! The darkness of evening
Falls as we sing before the sacred amina.
About us on all sides corn tassels are waving.
Hitciya yahina-a. The white light of day dawn
Yet finds us singing, while corn tassels are waving.
Hitciya yahina-a. The darkness of evening
Falls as we sing before the sacred amina.
About us on all sides corn tassels are waving.
Hitciya yahina-a. The white light of day dawn
Yet finds us singing, while the squash leaves are waving.

Hi-ihiya naiho-o! The earth is rumbling
From the beating of our basket drums.
The earth is rumbling from the beating
Of our basket drums, everywhere humming.
Earth is rumbling, everywhere raining.

Hi-ihiya naiho-o! Pluck out the feathers
From the wing of the Eagle and turn them
Toward the east where lie the large clouds.

Hitciya yahina-a. Pluck out the soft down
From the breast of the Eagle and turn it
Toward the west where sail the small clouds.
Hitciya yahina-a. Beneath the abode
Of the rain gods it is thundering;
Large corn is there. Hitciya yahina-a.
Beneath the abode of the rain gods
It is raining; small corn is there.

🌲 FIRST FRUITS CEREMONIES 🌲

Among the people of the Plateau, First Fruits ceremonies were held annually as each important food ripened. The Coeur d'Alene in northern Idaho celebrated when the service berries *(Amelanchier)* ripened. The Nez Percé observed both the ripening of the service berries and the blooming of the camas *(Camassia quamash)*, for when camas bloomed the roots were ready to dig. If the winter had been hard and last year's harvest meager, the people would have been very hungry, perhaps near starvation. At times, their only food would have been the black lichen that grows on pine trees—edible, but barely palatable. The ripening of native fruits was understandably cause for celebration. Whether service berries, camas roots, or bitterroot, the First Fruits ceremonies followed the same basic pattern: first, it was extremely important that no one should eat before the ceremony, or the spirits would be angry and the whole group would suffer. Next, the women dug enough camas for a meal for everyone. They piled some on a bark tray, and everyone gathered round. The leader offered this heaping tray of food to the principal deity or the Great Mystery, as it was sometimes known. After he had prayed and made the offerings, the people chanted prayers. The leader sang, and the people danced to the music of drums and rattles. As with many of the Green Corn or harvest dances, First Fruits dances were a form of prayer; not until the ceremony was completed would the people eat any of the new crop.

⚘ TOBACCO CEREMONIES ⚘

When the Hopi needed the help of the spirits, they offered tobacco, often along with sprinklings of cornmeal. The Menominee, Ojibwa, and Fox people offered dry tobacco leaves as a gift in exchange for some advantage or to turn away the wrath of whichever spirit might be responsible for their present predicament. Most people, except for the Karok of Northern California, seem never to have smoked tobacco merely for pleasure. Women seldom smoked unless they were shamans, or, in some tribes, if they were elderly. The Mohave and Hidatsa never smoked it, because they knew it caused shortness of breath and interfered with running. Nor would the Hidatsa plant it near corn because they believed tobacco had a strong smell that affected corn. Yet tobacco was almost universally a sacred plant, and its legendary origins reflect this. A version of a Cherokee myth of how people acquired tobacco goes like this:

When the world began, everyone shared one tobacco plant for all of their tobacco until the geese stole it and carried it far away. Without it, people suffered greatly. One old woman weakened so much that she was on the point of death. To save her life the animals tried to bring it back, but the geese saw each one and killed them before they could retrieve it. Even Mole tried, by burrowing underground, but the geese saw his track and killed him when he came out. At last Hummingbird said he would go. None of the geese saw him because he was tiny and quick. He darted down, snatched the top with the leaves and seeds, and was off again before the geese even knew he had been there. At home the old woman fainted and began to die, but Hummingbird arrived back just in time and blew smoke into her nostrils. With a shout of joy, she came alive and blessed Hummingbird for saving her life.

The Huron Feast of the Dead, held in the middle of winter when growing things sleep, often began with a tobacco invocation:

And again the tobacco smoke rises. We ask that it will continue in the same manner. That the wind will be just so strong that we are content. We are happy; the wind is just so strong that we are happy. And we ask that it will continue in the same manner in future days. And your mind will continue to be so.

Tobacco appears to have dominated the cultures of tribes from Northern California and southern Oregon, such as the Karok, Hupa, Yurok, Shasta, and Klamath. In Karok belief, tobacco came from the first people, the Ikxareyavs, who changed themselves into (among other things) animals, plants, mountains, and ideas. The Ikxareyavs had said that tobacco would be medicine. Because it numbed pain, people applied it as a poultice on painful areas, and used its leaves for toothache and earache. The Karok recognized two kinds of tobacco: "downslope" tobacco, and "real" tobacco (*Nicotiana bigelovii* var. *exaltata*). The Ikxareyavs had given both to the people, with instructions not to smoke the downslope, and to "feed the real tobacco to the Mountains." Because in Karok mythology the Ikxareyavs became mountains, the Karok believed they fed the Ikxareyavs tobacco when they planted it on slopes. But despite all the attention given to tobacco, there was relatively little ceremony in this tribe about planting, tending, or harvesting it—they simply collected the seed stalks and hung them in the rafters of the sweat house until it was time to plant in March, when the weeds had begun to sprout. As they sowed the seed in the ashes of burned oak logs on the hillsides, they prayed to it. Here is one such prayer:

Take this tobacco that I give thee, Mountain,
take and eat some of this, Mountain,
that I may be lucky.
May I live long.
May I have luck.
May I be able to buy a woman.

When the time came to cure, the gardeners separated the leaves from the stems and wrapped them in bracken fern to dry. They pounded both dry stems and leaves, but they considered the stem tobacco inferior to the leaf product. They saved the leaf tobacco for themselves to smoke and to sell, and offered the stem tobacco to low-class visitors. Likewise, no particular care was taken in storing stem tobacco, but for the leaf tobacco, nothing was too good. Women wove beautiful baskets in which to store it—baskets so attractive they were prized and traded widely both as baskets and as hats.

The Blackfeet believed they had received tobacco from the water spirits. It happened this way:

In the beginning, tobacco, or nawak'osis, was so secret that only four shamans knew of it. These men had all power, but the people had none, and there was no peace or unity in the tribe. A young man named Bull-By-Himself thought this was wrong, so he searched high and low for the plant. At last, some water spirits who had taken the form of beavers pitied him and his wife. They changed themselves into men in order to teach them the sacred songs, how to make the sacred pipes, and which dances and prayers to use. But when Bull-By-Himself and his wife had planted their tobacco garden, hail destroyed the garden of the four shamans, so that there was only one left. When Bull-By-Himself harvested the tobacco, he shared it with the other people, and the tribe knew peace and harmony because of nawak'osis. All tobacco seeds are descended from this very garden.

Because of this spiritual origin, the Blackfeet Tobacco Society divided tobacco crops with the rest of the people, so that everyone had some, but kept secret the methods of planting and harvesting. The gardens were so secret, in fact, that even members of the society dared not visit them after planting lest they disturb the Small People (imaginary folk something like leprechauns) who tended them while the group was on its summer bison hunt.

The Upper Kutenai had received their instructions to plant tobacco when the spirits appeared to one of their leaders in a dream. When he awoke, he said to the people, "Come, let us be on our way. The spirits say we must plant tobacco seeds." And so the people followed…to what is now Tobacco Plains, north of present-day Eureka, Montana.

4

THE FOUNDATION OF TRADE

B esides growing vegetables themselves, there were only two other means for native people to acquire them—trading and raiding. The anthropologist Frances Densmore in 1931 talked to northern Seminole people in present-day Florida, who still relished memories of the old days when they raided Creek farms in Georgia and Louisiana. Women may not have been among the raiders, but their role was significant. They produced the important trade commodities, corn and camas, and they were often the traders, especially when the produce was their own. And trading was not a result of European immigration to these shores—by the time Columbus arrived, it had been going on for centuries. At the time of Christ, Mesoamericans were growing corn, beans, squash, tomatoes, peanuts, and guavas. From there, these food plants, and tobacco, spread by trade to the northernmost latitude of North America that would support their growth.

Trade has been part of Indian culture, and garden plants have been an integral part of that trade, since well before the current millennium, and this trade was surprisingly widespread. Some items from the Pacific Coast made their way to Massachusetts, and other items from the eastern part of the continent were passed from hand to hand westward. In the Southwest, for instance, archaeologists have found pipes made of catlinite, a red stone quarried in Minnesota. When the French appeared in Iroquois territory in the early sixteenth century, people were trading corn and tobacco, along with sea-shells, pipes, and flint stones. They bartered these items and others with the surrounding tribes as well as among themselves, the members of the Iroquois Confederacy.

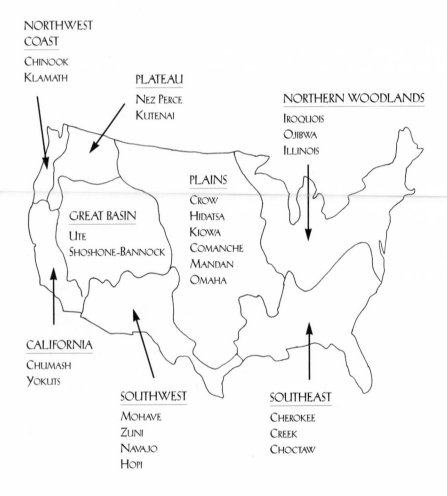

NORTHWEST
COAST
CHINOOK
KLAMATH

PLATEAU
NEZ PERCE
KUTENAI

NORTHERN WOODLANDS
IROQUOIS
OJIBWA
ILLINOIS

PLAINS
CROW
HIDATSA
KIOWA
COMANCHE
MANDAN
OMAHA

GREAT BASIN
UTE
SHOSHONE-BANNOCK

CALIFORNIA
CHUMASH
YOKUTS

SOUTHWEST
MOHAVE
ZUNI
NAVAJO
HOPI

SOUTHEAST
CHEROKEE
CREEK
CHOCTAW

The desire to trade led people to overcome great obstacles, both geographic and social (as they passed through hostile or enemy territory). The Mohave, who occupied the Lower Colorado, were instrumental in moving goods between the pueblos of eastern New Mexico and the California coast. Taking quantities of home-grown gourds, dried corn, cured tobacco, and war clubs, they crossed the Mohave Desert to trade with the Chumash, near present-day Santa Barbara and San Luis Obispo, and up the Sacramento Valley to the country of the Yokuts. Being fierce warriors, the Mohave feared no one in their path. Nonetheless, some tribes need not have made so formidable a journey merely for trade items; perhaps they were urged on by a sense of adventure, a desire to see far-off places. The Northern Kutenai, for example, grew tobacco near the Canadian border. They carried their tobacco and other trade goods on two- or three-year trading expeditions into Spanish territory. The arrival of the horse obviously made longer expeditions more feasible, but navigable rivers, strong canoes, and a sense of adventure may well have been of equal influence. (The horse itself became a trading comodity; the Nez Percé of eastern Washington were responsible for developing the desirable Appaloosa breed, which is still highly valued today.) Much of the long-distance trade described in this chapter occurred after the people acquired horses but before traditional patterns of life were permanently disrupted or destroyed by the arrival of large numbers of Europeans.

Accounts of early travelers give some idea of the obstacles encountered on any journey. Exploring Creek country in 1775, the naturalist William Bartram had a hair-raising midnight battle with an alligator that crawled out of a nearby swamp. Fortunately, he was on guard even in his sleep, and survived. Bartram was lucky to be nearly always in range of Indians who were generous with their hospitality, so he usually had enough to eat. Other travelers went hungry unless they could catch fish or kill game. Trails were often submerged during heavy rains. In winter, travelers floundered through belly-deep snow, and became ill from clothes that, once wet, stayed damp for weeks. They slogged through deep mud and choked in heavy dust. Flies and mosquitoes nearly drove them and their horses mad with their biting. To all of these hazards were added the grueling heat of the western deserts and the stifling humidity of the Plains. But despite all the hardships, trade was widespread throughout the continent, and at the center of it were foodstuffs. Some were garden produce: corn, beans, squash, sunflower seeds, and other vegetables, as well as tobacco. One primary food came from acceptance gardening—camas was popular on the Plains and in California, far from its origin in the Plateau area. These items were traded for (among other things) dried bison meat and hides, mocassins, other people's tobacco, slaves, and sea shells.

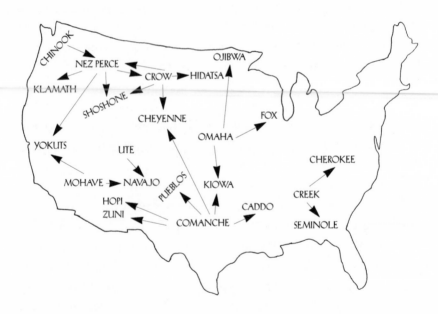

As people came together to trade, great trading centers sprang up. Lewis and Clark came upon one on their way to the Pacific

Ocean in the late autumn of 1804. They visited the Arikaras, in present-day South Dakota, then moved north to their business rivals, the Mandan and Hidatsa. There they found themselves at a regional center of Indian trade. Native people came from hundreds of miles to exchange trade goods for the vegetables these gardening tribes harvested, and other whites had already been trading with the Mandan since 1729. At the time of Lewis and Clark's visit, two hunting groups had traveled considerable distances to trade for provisions for winter. The Cheyenne had ridden up from their home country some 200 miles to the southwest. The Assiniboine had come down from their homes near the Canadian border. They and Lewis and Clark bartered with the Mandan and Hidatsa for corn, beans, dried squash, and sunflower seeds.

This was by no means the only trade center. At The Dalles on the Columbia River, a sort of giant American Indian shopping mall went on all summer. People came from what is now Washington, Northern California, the Great Basin (chiefly southern Idaho and eastern Oregon), British Columbia, and the Rocky Mountains. Here, goods were traded for items not available in the traders' homelands: from the Rockies came furs, dressed skins, and mountain goat wool. From the Plains came corn cakes, parched corn, dried squash, bison robes, and dried bison meat. From California came slaves, brought by the Modoc, who exchanged them for dentalia (see page 92). From the Plateau came dried salmon and camas cakes. The Coast people brought salmon and wapato roots, canoes, and woven articles, such as mats, baskets, and hats. Later came guns and iron implements—once such items became available, often in far-flung regions, they passed through many native trade routes long before the Europeans appeared in person. Often, trades at The Dalles were carried out through Indian middlemen such as the Nez Percé. The Nez Percé were major traders who often traveled from central Idaho to Canada, The Dalles, California, and the Plains. They traded with the Crow on the Plains, bringing back items such as bison robes and feather bonnets, which they had exchanged for camas cakes, dried salmon, dentalium shells, and horses. In the desert Southwest, people traded their corn and other garden produce with the more nomadic, nongardening bison hunters of the Plains. The Tewa, who lived in pueblos north of Santa Fe, traded with the Comanche, who came from Texas. The Comanche supplied bison hides and in exchange received corn, corn meal, and bread. It was a two-way trading relationship; the Comanche sometimes traveled to the pueblos, and trade representatives of the Tewa sometimes made the journey to Comanche territory. Consequently, the pueblo of Santa Clara became a primary trading center. Here, goods flowed into the Plains from as far away as Mexico and the Pacific Ocean.

East of the Mississippi, towns and villages were linked by a network of trails. Along these routes, native people both moved goods and hunted game. The Huron, who lived north of Lake Ontario, developed trade relationships with neighboring tribes north of the St. Lawrence, and with members of the Iroquois confederation south of the river. A gardening and fishing people, the Huron had their own produce and tobacco along with what they got from other tribes. They traded these together with fishing nets, wampum, and French goods that they exchanged for furs. The furs they then sold to the French fur traders. Wealth seems to have been approved of among the Huron, possibly because it showed hard work and the favor of the spirits. A wealthy person not only could be generous and hospitable to others, but was *expected* to display these traits.

To the south, the Creek and Cherokee, besides being great gardeners, were also renowned traders. The Creeks built large, seagoing canoes of cypress trunks, and in them they sailed down the coast of Florida to the Bahamas and even to Cuba, where they traded for Caribbean tobacco, sugar, and (as William Bartram put it) "spiritous liquors" (probably rum). Bartram mentions being offered a choice piece of tobacco that the Creek trader said had come from the governor of Cuba. In addition to the American garden trio, the Creeks traded hickory nut oil, honey, beeswax, and medicinal herbs to other native people in western Florida and Georgia. To the French they traded vegetables and game meats, as well as their handicrafts. The Creeks used trade as a kind of welfare system. Gardening gave employment to widows and old people, and in exchange for their vegetables they received life's necessities. Bartram recalls being told by a leader of one Creek village that plows were not acceptable for trading because they were too efficient—they would put the needy out of work.

With the coming of the English traders, economy boomed for the Creeks, who eagerly adapted to new imports such as chocolate, coffee, and sugar. They expanded their gardens with apples, peaches, and other crops, and became famous for their horticulture. When deerskin clothing became fashionable among men in Europe, the Creek economy exploded—they became among the chief suppliers of deerskins for that market. The deerskin trade gave them more money with which to purchase hard goods such as iron tools. (A broad hoe, for example, cost three deerskins.) In addition, there were different sorts of knives, axes, and hatchets for varied purposes. By the early colonial period, the Natchez-Texas trail linked present-day Natchez, Mississippi, with the Rio Grande and settlements in Mexico. The Menomini, from the area west of Lake Michigan, traded with the Ojibwa and with the Santee Sioux in what is now southern Minnesota. The Fox traded with both the Menominee and the Ojibwa for wild rice. The Omaha journeyed from present-day eastern Nebraska up to northern Minnesota to trade for iron implements with the Ojibwa and the French at Lake Winnipeg. At these points of east-west contact and at others, trade items flowed back and forth.

The Omaha seem to have been particularly well traveled. They knew about the Rocky Mountains, were familiar with the Black Hills of Dakota, and were in fairly regular contact with the Crow. Through their close connections, the Ponca, they were acquainted with the Nez Percé. Their trade contacts with the Ojibwa led to some cultural interchange—similarities developed between the Omaha Shell Society and the Mide Wi'win (Grand Medicine) Society of the Ojibwa. Both taught that evil shortened life, as it had a bad effect on the evildoer. The Menomini also had wide connections among people outside their own neighborhood. These people lived in northern Minnesota in an area where three types of economy came together: the western game area, the northern wild-rice area, and the eastern and southern agricultural area. People from any of these areas bent on trade passed through their territory by boat or canoe on the lakes and up and down the rivers.

🌲 CIRCLES OF TRADE WEST OF THE MISSISSIPPI 🌲

Because archaeologists cannot really determine whether a nine-hundred-year-old kernel of corn came from a local area or was traded from hundreds of miles away, trade relationships are more readily interpreted from hard goods such as sea shells. So the story of the circle of trade in the West begins on the western coast of Vancouver Island, where the Pacific Ocean meets the North American continental shelf. Here, on the ocean floor 50–150 feet below the surface, lives a small mollusk called a dentalium *(Dentalium pretiosum)*. Perhaps an inch or two long, and less than half an inch around, dentalia shells served many native people, particularly in Northern California, as money. A string of dentalia was six inches long, and the fewer the dentalia on it (i.e., the bigger the shells), the more valuable it was. A string with eleven dentalia was worth about fifty dollars. A string of fifteen was worth about two dollars, fifty cents. To possess clothing decorated with these shells set a person off from the crowd as someone of substance. The more shells on a garment, the wealthier the person was. Covering hats or collars or even dresses and shirts with the shells, so that they seemed to be made only of shells, proved that the wearer had great standing among his or her people as well as with the spirits. Like other commodities, scarcity increased value, so the shells were worth more in California or along the Mississippi than they were in the Pacific Northwest. Because they could only be harvested in one small area and with great difficulty, dentalia shells retained their value in the native economy, by some estimations, for more than twenty-five hundred years. Originating with the Nootka or the Ehattesaht and Quatsino (accounts vary), the dentalia passed to the Makah, a tribe that still lives on the spot where the Pacific meets the Strait of Juan de Fuca. From there, they reached the Chinook, whose location at the mouth of the Columbia River allowed them to control Columbia River trade, which made them the premier traders of the Northwest Coast. The Chinook carried the shells up the Columbia to The Dalles, and traded them, as well as other coastal goods, with the Nez Percé and the Klamath for camas cakes and other items from very far away.

Certain areas in which the camas bulb was widespread became gathering places for area tribes. One was Camas Prairie, north of the Snake River in central Idaho. This was the territory of the Shoshone and their close connections, the Bannock from southwestern Montana. During the gathering season, in May, neighboring tribes came from many miles around. Any hostilities were suspended, as the women set to work digging enough bulbs for the family's immediate and long-range needs, and for trade. The Nez Percé often gathered at Camas Prairie to dig camas with the Northern Shoshoni. Although not so large a trade mall as The Dalles, Camas Prairie was central to Great Basin trade. The Shoshone and Bannock, by sharing their camas grounds with other tribes, reaped trade benefits for themselves. They traded not only with the Nez Percé, but with the Klamath in southeastern Oregon and the Crow. Another camas-digging ground lay not far from the falls of the Spokane River, in what is now eastern Washington. It often became a smaller version of The Dalles during camas season, as the tobacco-growing Upper Kutenai came from the northern Rockies to dig bulbs or trade for them. The Upper Kutenai were great traders. In his account of life among the Piegan Blackfeet in the mid nineteenth century, James Willard Schultz describes a trading visit by the Kutenai who came to trade with the Piegans (one of the three tribes in the Blackfeet confederacy). They brought arrowroot and camas, which Schultz describes as a "sticky, sweet, yellowish" cake. It was very welcome after a long time without vegetables of any sort.

Nez Percé traders traveled eastward to trade with the Crow, southward into Ute territory, and southwest into Northern California. Sometimes, they were joined by the Kutenai on these expeditions, but it is not clear if both groups continued on into Spanish territory, as the Kutenai are said to have done. When traveling east, the Nez Percé used the Lolo Trail, which crossed the Rockies from the north fork of Clearwater River over Lolo Pass near central Idaho.

On the Plains, the Crow were middlemen between the Nez Percé and the Kutenai; the Mandan, Hidatsa, and Arikara to the east; the Blackfeet to the north; and the southern Plains people such as the Cheyenne, Arapaho, and Kiowa. Lewis and Clark, when they arrived in 1805, found the Crow actively trading with the Hidatsa. The explorers recorded that the Crow had been acquiring nonnative goods from the Mandan and Hidatsa, but had never before traded with white people directly.

From southeastern Washington, the Nez Percé and the Walla Walla traveled into central California on a well-defined trading route known as the Walla Walla Trail. Along the way, they passed through (and probably traded with) tribes who also were accustomed to traveling to The Dalles: the Cayuse (from northwestern Oregon), the Klamath (from southern Oregon), and the Modoc. Beyond Mount Shasta, their venture took them through the territories of the Achumawi and the Yuki. Finally, they rode through Maidu and Miwok lands into Yokuts country, in what is now the

Sacramento Valley. This is where the Walla Walla Trail ended. Many of these tribes (the Yurok, Modoc, Hupa, and Karok) had a money economy. Unlike the Plains tribes, who valued dentalia as decoration, the Northern California people (specifically the Karok and the Yurok) used dentalia only as money. In fact, dentalia money dominated Karok culture, a culture with a strict observance of gender roles: the men hunted, fished, grew tobacco, and harvested acorns, the main vegetable food. Once the food was harvested, the women owned it, and the men had to buy food back from the women with money. They might not even know how much food the women had. But since men controlled the tobacco, any woman who wanted to smoke had to buy tobacco from the men. One dentalia shell, depending on its length, would buy, roughly, a woman's cap full of tobacco.

The Mohave were an important link in the western circle of trade, for they supplied corn, beans, dried pumpkin, and gourd seeds to the Yokuts, the Chumash, and the Navajo and other Southwestern people. Through the agency of the Mohave—and perhaps others—goods were carried into present-day Arizona and New Mexico. This trade may have been established as early as 900 A.D., when the Mohave followed a trade trail that extended between northern Arizona and the Pacific Coast, across the Mohave Desert. Another east/west trail began in southern Arizona on the Gila River, crossed the desert to the northwest, then ran up the Coachella Valley near present-day San Bernardino. It is not known for certain whether or not the Mohave ever encountered northern tribes in the country of the Yokuts or the Chumash, but the Mohave, Nez Percé, and Walla Walla all appear to have traded with the Yokuts. The Mohave were well positioned to travel between California peoples and those in northern Arizona.

The Navajo's location in the high deserts of northern Arizona and New Mexico in turn appears to have made them a hub for trade in all directions. The Navajo traded with Utes to the north, the Spanish to the south, the Mohave and others to the east, and the Pueblos in the west. An agricultural people, they grew corn, beans, squash, and other produce. These and other commodities, such as pine nuts, they offered for trade. The Comanche, likewise, were ideally situated to be the hub of a great trading wheel. Their own territory, in what is now western Texas, put them in range of the Kiowa to the north, the Pueblos to the west, the Wichita to the east, and various Apache groups to the south and southwest. The Comanche hunted rather than gardening. Like some groups of the Sioux, they preferred to trade (or raid) for necessities of life other than bison. They were good businessmen and sharp traders—so good, in fact, that after the arrival of the Spanish, trade built up between Comanche leaders and Mexican traders. This economic relationship became known as the comanchero trade, and the Comanche were able to maintain it for more than 250 years. As the settlers from the east began moving into Texas and competing with the Mexicans for markets, the Comanche played both ends against the middle for their own advantage.

The eastern Pueblos—those living in the Rio Grande Valley of northern New Mexico—were producing corn, beans, pumpkins, gourds, cotton, and tobacco before the Spaniards arrived. These and other commodities they exported to the Navajo and the Hopi in the west and the Comanche in the east, as well as to neighboring Apache, Mescalero, and Jicarilla. After they came on the scene, the Spanish joined in the trade, too. The Tewa trade seems to have been fairly typical of the Pueblos. They traded corn and corn products for bison meat and hides with the Comanche and with neighboring Apache. Although the Tewa lived in permanent communities, they sometimes traveled with their produce and clay pots to the Comanche. Other times, the Comanche came to them. A trade fair similar to that at The Dalles became established at the pueblos of Taos and Santa Clara. People came from all over the desert Southwest and the southern Plains. The Hopi left their mesas and crossed Navajo territory to bring woolens and corn to exchange for bison products. The Apache ate their green corn, then traded bison products for mature corn and seed corn with the eastern pueblos.

Archaeological finds show that after the thirteenth century, the most important commodities in trade between the Plains and the Pueblos were foodstuffs, although from the beginning turquoise jewelry, shells, and other manufactured items were evident. By the beginning of the sixteenth century, bison products had become vital, and perhaps as a result the southern Plains people turned to hunting and gathering, and traded for foods to complete their nutritional needs. Corn and squash, in particular, were exchanged for meat. From the point of view of the Pueblos, hunting for large game animals was time-consuming and difficult, sometimes involving long journeys away from home. Once the animal had been killed and dressed out, there was the problem of transporting it home again. The payback for these trips was often not worth the risk when people could fulfill their need for meat protein by the relatively less difficult (and more fun) method of trading for it. Then as now, people enjoyed trying new commodities, such as new blends of tobacco. The Tewa cultivated the *Nicotiana attenuata*, which grows in the Southwest, and mixed it with a local sumac, *Rhus cismontana*. (Sumac supposedly induced a mildly lethargic reaction.) The Kiowa, whose territory lay north of the Comanche south of the Platte River in southern Kansas and northern Oklahoma, mixed their tobacco with a different species of sumac, *R. glabra* (smooth upland sumac). Both the Kiowa and the Crow had elaborate and complex beliefs and rituals surrounding the cultivation and harvesting of tobacco. When these people met, it is entirely possible that they exchanged more than commodities— some of their beliefs about tobacco, and the greater emphasis they gave its cultivation, were similar. In addition, the Kiowa purchased sundance weed *(Croton texensis)*, a plant used in the Sun Dance, from the Crow.

Wherever native people gathered to trade, the occasion was marked by ceremony and celebration, whether it involved two or three tribes or several, as at The Dalles, Taos, or Camas Prairie. At times, two or more tribes might be at war with each other when they came together to trade; other tribes were, at best, business rivals. Such shifting relationships were common, so a trade customarily began with a smoke. If hostilities had to be suspended, as was often the case, a smoke sealed the negotiations and signaled everyone's agreement to not fight each other until business was concluded. When the Cheyenne wanted to acquire Hidatsa corn, the men first had to conclude a truce. If people were meeting for the first time, a smoke served to let everyone know that the parties who wanted to trade were people of honest heart and straight dealing. A secondary benefit of this preliminary smoke was the opportunity for the men to sample each other's tobacco.

After peace was declared, women and children brought out their produce. The women were agressive traders, as Alexander Henry discovered. Henry was a Northwest Company fur trader, who first encountered the Mandan or Hidatsa (he wasn't sure which) about five years after Lewis and Clark. He wrote:

> They soon asked us to trade, and brought buffalo robes, corn, beans, dried squashes, etc.; but we informed them we did not come here for that purpose, merely to visit them and see the country. They could not comprehend why we should have come so far out of mere curiosity, and said that all white people who came there did so with a view to trade. They suspected that we had goods which we wished to take over the river to other villages, and were anxious to prevent it. We purchased sweet corn, beans, meal, and various other trifles, for which we paid in ammunition, beads, and tobacco. [We were] plagued by the women and girls, who continued to bring bags and dishes full of different kinds of produce and insisted upon trading.

These occasions were an opportunity to have fun, too. Boys and young men played their favorite ball games, and learned new games from others. They raced their horses to show off what their animals could do. (Everywhere they were shown, the Nez Percé Appaloosas were prized more than any other horse.) They sampled different foods, which were offered both for sale and for hospitality. There might be variously flavored corn cakes, seasoned with unfamiliar herbs or with salt from an unfamiliar salt bed. There was hickory milk (from the Creek) or goat's milk (Navajo). There were sunflower cakes and meat delicacies. Some people cured pemmican in the smoke of juniper. Others preferred cedar, while still others used sweet grass *(Hierochloe odorata)* from northern Montana. In addition, every lodge or camp had food in constant preparation, and it was a matter of courtesy to feed whoever asked. Anyone could dip into a cooking pot and help themselves—within limits. All day people danced. Drums beat, clam shells and (after European contact) bells tinkled, and reed flutes and whistles were piped for social dances. Gambling games of all sorts went on. People bet on anything—which horse would win, or which scorpion would kill the other. Variations on the bones game parted men and women from their goods. (The bones used were the vertebrae of creatures such as birds or rabbits or snakes, which people took turns tossing into a circle.) New friendships were formed, alliances were made and broken, fights broke out and were settled, and love was made and lost. The air was thick with wood smoke, cooking odors, garbage, passion, and profit. When trading was done, it would be time to start home. If they had been effective traders, the family or the tribe or the village would eat, or at least not starve, until the next good hunt or harvest. If they went away with little, at least they had perhaps eaten well for a few days.

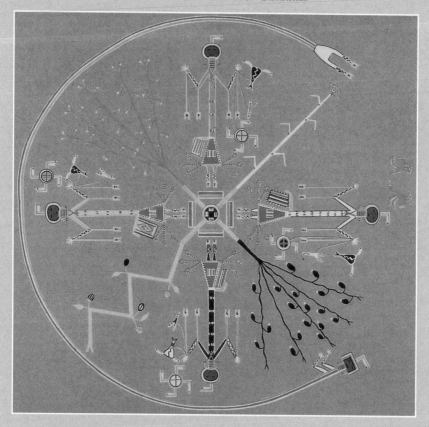

In the Navajo's Mountain Chant rituals, a large sand painting was drawn on the floor of the medicine lodge. It took about seven hours to complete, and was sometimes used in conjunction with a myth. One such myth, which can be found on page 67 and accompanies this painting, describes how the four sacred plants were gifts from four bears.

ABOVE: *In this sand painting, the four sacred plants are growing from a center of pollen outward toward the four sacred directions. White corn is in the east, blue squash is in the west, yellow beans are in the south, and black tobacco is in the north. From the center rise four cloud columns, and surrounding it all is the Rainbow Girl, open to the east.*

BELOW: *This Navajo sand painting is from the Hail Chant. Rain Boy and Rain Girl walk sunwise around a central lake surrounded by clouds with dragonflies on them. Between the clouds are the four sacred plants: corn, beans, squash, and tobacco. Rain Boy carries lightning and a sun ray, and he travels on lightning; Rain Girl carries rain-rope and a sun ray, and she travels on rainbows.*

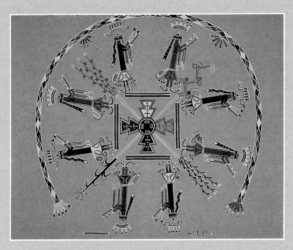

5
TRADITION REGAINED

By the end of the nineteenth century, American Indians were struggling to maintain their rich gardening traditions. Beginning in 1831, the Five Civilized Tribes—the Choctaw, Chickasaw, Cherokee, Creek, and the Seminole—were removed from their ancestral homes in the southeast to make room for white settlers who wanted their lands. Even after traveling the Trail of Tears, and settling anew in what is now the state of Oklahoma, they faced renewed and constant pressure to give up the lands they had acquired there. Yet so skillful were these people at growing crops that by 1833, after being removed from "guaranteed" lands for the second time, the Choctaw had already produced a surplus of forty thousand bushels of corn.

On the Plains, the slaughter of more than five million bison destroyed half of the Indian economic base. In the West, native people were rapidly being confined to reservations where they were made dependent both on the good will of the government and on the honesty of Indian agents to make certain they received what the treaties promised them. With the demise of the bison and the loss of their freedom to travel, their economy collapsed. And on February 8, 1887, Congress passed the Dawes Severalty Act, which nearly gave the American Indian gardening tradition the coup de grâce. As disasters sometimes do, it began with good intentions. Many well-intentioned whites thought the best solution for Indians was assimilation into the general population. Congress seems to have thought that granting each native person some land to own individually would make them independent and self-sufficient. The Dawes Act therefore granted each married man a meager 160 acres. Each single man over the age of eighteen received eighty acres, and each male child received forty acres. The purpose of these grants was, on the surface, to empower Indians to become self-sufficient farmers. In reality, they were a vehicle to wrest thousands of acres of reservation land away from them. In the nineteenth century and well into the twentieth, farming was the primary way to make a living in the United States and its territories. Congressman Dawes and others thought that farming would suit the American Indians who had had an agricultural tradition, and that those who did not could learn. But as white pioneers discovered, even 640 acres was often inadequate to earn a good living for a family from farming.

There were several problems with the government's approach. First of all, it failed to consider the difficult conditions of western farming. The West is predominantly an arid region; much of it receives less than ten inches of rainfall per year. Even on the West Coast, available water is heavily dependent upon annual mountain snowpacks. The wind blows constantly over the Great Plains, sometimes with devastating results—as people discovered during the drought of the 1930s when thousands of tons of topsoil blew away. None of the Plains gardening people, who had grown surplus vegetables for hundreds of years, had ever gardened anywhere except near water. The Mandan, Hidatsa, and Arikara, for instance, had their gardens on the banks of the Missouri, not on the bluffs above. Had Congress asked these people about conditions on the

Plains, the European pioneers might have been forewarned about the often heartbreaking difficulties. Second, the Dawes Act did not recognize the precarious nature of farming even under the best of conditions. Droughts, freezes, floods, diseases, and pests all affect farming, to say nothing of market conditions. Primarily, however, the Dawes Act was destined for failure because it did not consider native cultural differences. Many native cultures believed (and still do believe) that it is a heinous crime to use a plow to carve up the flesh of their mother, Earth. Nomadic bison hunters could not simply make a change overnight to a way of life for which they had no training, no knowledge, and no tradition. A modern corollary is the difficulty of making democratic reforms in Russia, which has never known democracy.

Many native people realized quickly that for them to depend solely on farming as a means of earning a living was to invite disaster. Even when they had had control over their own destinies, with their economy balanced between hunting, gardening, and trading, they were often hungry and sometimes close to starvation. Now, they were driven to accepting an economic pattern foreign to them. Congress completely misunderstood the native agricultural tradition, which was based on gardening, not farming. The grouping of small plots together for safety, convenience, and sociability gave casual observers the impression that native people farmed on a much larger scale than they actually did. These small intensive gardens yielded so much produce in good years that travelers often thought the cultivated acreage had to be much larger than it actually was.

Congress also fatally misinterpreted the native cultural patterns surrounding gardening. It allocated farmland only to men, and assumed that men would be responsible for the farms. It blithely assumed that if men did not know how to farm, they could learn. In making these assumptions and removing women from agriculture altogether, Congress overlooked centuries of gardening knowledge possessed by women. Women had been responsible for half of their tribes' indigenous economy, as they were the primary gardeners and usually the produce traders. With a grand Victorian disregard for reality, Congress considered all women (native or European) too frail for farming and sought to replace them with men on the grounds that heavy farm work was unsuitable for women. Women were to cook and clean and bring up children.

By allocating individual plots of land, the Dawes Act violated the communal nature of Indian work and child rearing, which was social rather than individual. The Mandans believed that Good Fur Robe had formed the Goose Women Society to benefit all of the people. This society performed rituals designed to ensure that there would be plenty of corn and other vegetables, that the children would be healthy, and the young men would be successful in war. The women in this society worked together for the good of the tribe. Similarly, Iroquois women viewed gardening as a communal effort. For them, as for most avid gardeners, gardening was fun, not drudgery. In teaching their children how to plant corn and other vegetables, the mothers made a game of it, and the little ones happily joined in. It was an opportunity to teach children that everyone's contribution was important, and that the people needed everyone's efforts in order to survive. The Dawes Act sought to impose European ideas of land ownership on native people who had never viewed land in that way.

Cheating was rampant. Once a man had accepted his allotment, unscrupulous whites often persuaded him to sell, and he was left with nothing but a few dollars. By 1934 the flaws in the Dawes Act were obvious and Congress passed the Wheeler-Howard bill, also known as the Indian Reorganization Act. This act mandated native organization into tribes, with self-government by tribal councils. It also sought to improve education and establish an Indian court. It abolished allotments, restored surplus lands to the tribes, and set up a two-million-dollar annual fund to buy new lands. Its philosophy promoted communal rather than private

property, and its goal was to help the Indians become self-support-
ing and survive on their own ethnic terms.

First they had to have enough to eat. Working with the
County Extension services in the land grant (agricultural) col-
leges, the Bureau of Indian Affairs (BIA) had already established a
two-fold agricultural effort in farming and gardening. The farming effort give native people a place in the American economy by
providing each family with a means of earning a living, but gardening would ensure that they could put food on the
table—whether or not the farm paid its way. Because gardening
was lighter work in that it did not require handling a plow while
guiding a horse or a team of horses, it once more became part of
the sphere of women. Unfortunately, after the onslaught of the
previous forty years, much of their gardening knowledge had
been lost, except for a few people such as Nodinens or Buffalo
Bird Woman, the Hidatsa gardener. The generation of old women
who had known the gardening ways of their people was disap-
pearing fast, and with them a valuable repository of the people's
gardening knowledge.

During the late 1920s and 1930s, in an ironic reversal of history, white women, working as home economists, taught
gardening to Indian women, while white men, themselves farmers, took jobs as farm agents and taught farming to Indian men.
Each agent was required to write a report to their superiors, in
which the agent set out his goals for the following year, reported
on how well the goals of the previous year had been met, and
wrote a narrative of the successes and problems in his jurisdiction.
The reports cited here from the thirties reflect the problems that
were faced in carrying out these assignments. The weather was a
constant foe—it was either too dry or too wet or too cold. Pests
were a severe problem, especially grasshoppers and weevils. One
year, tomato blight killed all the tomatoes for an entire reservation.
Skilled farmers though these men were, they were not always well
educated; writing reports came hard to people who were more

adept at holding the reins of a team than a pen. Seeing the conditions in which native people lived, they often became advocates for the people. The farm agent for the Choctaw of Mississippi, descendants of people who had refused to be removed from their lands, described the terrible weather in 1935:

> I landed here on Feb. 1st, 1935, just after a heavy snow, for this section, had fallen and melted off. It then set in to raining, and all the low lands was covered with several feet of water, and did not dry up enough to farm until along in the later part of May. The upland was plowed and most of it planted to cotton in its season. A part of my District is hill land, and not very well adapted to the raising of corn, and has to be fertilized well before it will produce a crop of any kind. This is costly and very few of the Indians are able to buy it in quantities enough to make it a paying proposition from a commercial standpoint, and you have to have moisture, or it won't make then, this happened here this year, after the rains stopped it turned off dry, and all crops was cut in half. In one of my communities nearly all the Indians were in open revolt, against the Superintendent, the Government, and with most anyone connected with the Government, this made it hard for a new man to get started, but the situation is some better at this time. I drafted a program after I had looked the situation over, and did not set up a definite goal for them. It is my intention to take this very same program up again during the coming year, and see if it can be worked out, after this one failure, which was not my fault, nor the fault of the Indians, or the Superintendent, we did our part, but was not able to control the weather, and we live in hopes that the coming year will deal more favorably with us all.

Besides the weather, they had to contend with the government's system of regulating the amount of crops they could plant. The farm agent's primary goal was to enable thirty Indians to raise enough corn and other products to last them for feed and food until another crop could be made. It was necessary to make some kind of arrangements to provide some of them with feed and food to make this crop with. Our funds was small, so we was not able to give them what they needed. To offset this we gave them work to do, paid them wages for building roads, and by so doing managed to help them out in a way, but not as much as we would have liked to do. Some pure seed corn was bought, and in one or two places it made good, but did not average up all over. Very few had feed to work their stock on, and those that planted cotton in the small amounts allowable under the Government setup was able to get a small seed loan, this was mostly used to buy feed, and fertilizer. This fertilizer was used chiefly on the cotton, in order to make it produce enough to pay the loan back, and the corn, and other food crops did not make very well. The drouth then set in, and most of the corn died for want of moisture, some fields did not make the seed back that was planted thereon, and I only know of two Indian farmers in my district who made enough corn to feed them until they can make another crop. The small amount of land that the farmers are now allowed to plant to cotton, which is the only cash crop that is planted, hardly justifies them to plant it, as the cost of production gives them very little for their labor. I set as my goal to try and get one Indian family in each of my communities to plant one acre to garden. After looking over most of the places that are used here for gardens, I saw that I had made a mistake. Nearly all the Indians have a small plot fenced off that is used for a place to grow early maturing varieties of vegetables, and will have several more places around over their farms where they will plant something in the vegetable line, just where they have a place that is rich enough to grow something, is where it will be planted, it may be right in the middle of his corn field, or along the edge of some reed brake, but he knows where it will grow, and there is where he plants it.

Out of his own wages, the agent himself bought sweet potato seed and raised several thousand plants, which he gave away to all who wanted them. The potatoes fared rather well, despite the drought, but they had worse luck with tomatoes, which died in the summer. Nevertheless, the Choctaw gardening tradition seems to have kept the people from starving. They grew turnips, sweet potatoes, peas, and beans, and despite problems with weevils, most people had food until spring. These people impressed the farm agent with the yield from their gardens. In a 1933 report, he noted that just forty-six acres of gardens yielded: 19,020 pounds of potatoes, 7,010 pounds of onions, 2,620 pounds of squash, 12,150 pounds of cabbage, 13,380 pounds of tomatoes, 48,100 pounds of rutabaga or turnips, and 32,340 pounds of dry beans. Corn, being considered a farm crop rather than a garden crop, was not included in this report, but the people produced 16,245 bushels of shelled corn. The agent also notes that the people "complain of worn-out soils. They say they can no longer, 'as did our fathers' move on to virgin soil." He reported that his goals had been reached: "Every family had plenty to eat."

Among the Five Civilized Tribes who had relocated to Oklahoma, the report for 1932 had as a goal to have fourteen hundred Indian families growing a well-balanced garden of sufficient size to furnish food throughout the year. The result: 2,860 planted gardens, of which nearly all produced food for the family during the garden season. This report shows how people could sometimes use the gardens to better their overall economic conditions as well as get enough to eat. The government had set up a program of awarding a cow or a brood sow to the gardener who grew the best garden. A Chickasaw woman won first prize—a cow—for her garden. In a 1931 report, "a man with no allotment won enough first prizes in agriculture [from his garden] to buy and pay for ten acres in land."

In addition to problems with the weather and pests, gardeners often had to contend with bureaucratic inefficiency and broken promises that were worse than natural disasters. At the Fort Hall Reservation in southern Idaho, among the Shoshone-Bannock, the farm agent could hardly contain his rage in his 1935 report:

> The garden phase of this project suffered a relapse this year. Garden seed had been promised by the IERA (Indian Emergency Relief Agency) and Indians were told that seed would be available from this source. The usual emphasis was placed on the importance of gardens as providing a large part of the family living at minimum cost and it was expected that the acreage of gardens would show an appreciable increase over other years. Many Indians prepared their ground and waited for seed till planting time was nearly past; then many of them lacked means of obtaining seed for the gardens they expected to have. The number of gardens that can be called by the name without too severe a strain on the imagination has been placed at 250 with a total acreage of 70.

In eastern Washington, on the Colville Reservation, the people had no previous gardening tradition, but by 1940 they had adapted to the need to grow their own food. Then the construction of Grand Coulee Dam, completed in 1942, flooded much of the good land. One of the best gardeners had to start all over: "...he moved and made a new garden. He selected a plot in a low place near a small spring for the garden and diverted water from the spring to the garden by means of troughs so that the vegetables could be irrigated. This fall he gathered and stored feed and vegetables enough to run him throughout the year."

During the Great Depression, the failure rate of the family farm reached an all-time high, and white farmers abandoned their farms to the banks and fled to California. Native people did not have that option; they were tied to the reservations where their people lived. In western Washington, where no gardening tradition had existed, the county extension and farm agents tried to establish one. To encourage people to supplement their income and their diet with gardening, one community worker helped found a club and held a contest with prizes for the best garden and the best display of canned goods. The same worker organized a women's club that included gardening. The women prepared the ground by hand with a shovel, and the agency gave them the seed. Another windfall came in the form of discarded furniture and army uniforms from Fort Lewis, near Tacoma. This gave the worker the idea for a garden contest with furniture as prizes for the best gardens. She made score cards that listed all the points for which people could earn credit. Although more points earned better prizes, everyone won something so that no one would be discouraged. The gardens were judged when they were at their best. Finally, she established a cannery and taught the people how to use pressure cookers. People brought in fruit and vegetables from their gardens and from the wild. Some people had secret places where they found wild blackberries that grew low to the ground on prickly vines. The women also canned hundreds of pounds of the salmon that were readily available around Puget Sound.

Despite the sincere efforts of this worker and other people like her, however, success only lasted during the time that she was there to provide motivation. Few people now garden on that reservation; gardening is just too difficult to establish among people whose culture did not ever have a gardening tradition. Once the motivation was gone, the people ceased to garden because it was much easier to buy food at area grocery stores. The Kiowa, on the other hand, did have a gardening tradition and the experience of a woman who worked among the Kiowa was much different. In 1935, Miss Smith reported that 96 percent of the families she worked with planted gardens along the creeks. Although the farm agent complained in his annual report that the people neglected their farms to observe traditional celebrations and dances, Miss Smith encouraged the members of her Women's Club to sing traditional songs as part of "music appreciation." She also encouraged tribal arts and crafts.

At best, resettlement in a foreign environment and retraining in alien techniques seriously disrupted gardening skills. The Navajo had been decimated by an armed troop led by Kit Carson in 1863–1864 and forced to walk three hundred miles south to Basque Redondo, New Mexico—a journey seared into their memory as the Long Walk. There they were held for five years until the United States government sent them home in 1868 with $100,000 worth of sheep and equipment. Very few Navajo people garden today. The Choctaw had been such skillful gardeners that they managed, despite two forced removals, to produce large quantities of corn. But European farming methods were failing all over the Great Plains, for whites and Native people alike. Straight-row plowing, the pride of the white farmer, helped create the Dust Bowl. Thousands of tons of irreplaceable top soil blew away during the depression drought from white-owned farms and Indian reservations alike. The Dust Bowl taught farmers about contour plowing, which prevents soil erosion. In later years, farmers' heavy use of commercial fertilizers, insecticides, and herbicides has fouled streams and polluted ground water. Now, however, there is a turn toward sustainable agriculture among European-American farmers as well as American Indians, and gardening is part of this agrarian revolution for both.

Sustainable agriculture is the use of techniques for farming and gardening that enable the farmer to make a good living by growing good food on healthy land. Or, as a current phrase puts it, sustainable agriculture uses techniques that are "economically viable, environmentally sound, and socially acceptable." Many of these techniques were well known to previous generations of both white and Native cultures. For Native people, renewed interest in the techniques of their ancestors comes from a desire for self-determination. Gradually, they are taking control of their destiny into their own hands, away from the federal government. They look back to a time when they were self-sustaining, and adapt ancient techniques to modern conditions. Two such programs, led and directed by Indians, are the Zuni Sustainable Agriculture Project and the Navajo New Dawn Project. Each contains a gardening project with the aim of teaching people how to provide enough food for themselves and their families.

The Navajo Project was begun in 1981. It emphasizes hands-on gardening from the ground up, and teaches people how to prepare the soil, and how to plant garden crops and fruit trees. It educates people about fertilizers and irrigation methods, and offers canning workshops and other classes such as how to make pickles and jam. A significant part of the educational effort looks at the past. The project teaches about native foods and plants—what the people ate and survived on during famines or conflicts. They collect information from elders and teach it to the younger generation from preschool through high school. Some of the meetings might include a presentation on the harvest time for such native plants as sumac, Navajo tea, or berries. For knowledge that lies outside the Navajo tradition, such as landscaping or the care of trees, they call on outside services such as the United States Forest Service.

The Zuni Sustainable Agriculture Project (ZSAP) defines sustainable agriculture as "farming in ways that provide a good return for farmers' work today, while protecting and improving soil, water, crops and other natural resources for future generations. It also means that local people and their communities are in control, and that the farming is based on their cultural values and benefits them economically, nutritionally, and socially." For Zuni people, the term "sustainability" has an additional dimension beyond its agricultural meaning; they are interested in exploring the science of gardening. Together with New Mexico State University, ZSAP conducts experiments to determine which corn hybrids grow best when planted at different depths, in dry land or when irrigated, and in finer or coarser soil.

The Zuni Sustainable Agriculture Garden Project (ZSAGP) promotes organic gardening methods among local farmers and gardeners, at ZSAGP headquarters, at the Ashiwi Awan Museum and Heritage Center in Zuni, and in schools. ZSAGP gardeners have assisted in planting gardens at Zuni elementary schools, working with the teachers to teach children traditional planting methods. They give presentations to classes, and encourage the children to take care of the plants. These gardeners are bringing back the traditional waffle gardens, which have been out of use for some years. A waffle garden is composed of any number of connecting squares, some about two feet by two feet, others four by four, but size is not significant in these gardens. The important thing about a waffle garden is to mound up the dirt around the planting space in each square to keep water in. ZSAGP gardeners have been instrumental in constructing model waffle gardens that demonstrate how to grow traditional Zuni garden plants. At the Museum and Heritage Center in Zuni, senior citizens, project gardeners, and high school students have cooperated in constructing two traditional waffle gardens, approximately twenty feet long by ten feet wide. One garden is composed of smaller squares; the other of larger ones. An adobe wall and a stick fence surround these gardens, to show how traditional waffle gardens were protected from larger pests such as donkeys. High school students have also made a model of the garden, complete with plants, to show how these traditional gardens were used.

At ZSAGP headquarters, the gardens are larger, perhaps fifty feet by twenty feet. The gardeners have planted several types of corn—Taos corn, Zuni corn, blue corn, and popping corn—along with beans, watermelons, cabbage, tomatoes, cilantro, and other crops. The waffle design lets a gardener flood each square once in several days, depending on the rate of soil percolation and the surface air temperature. In this garden, despite the unusual heat (above ninety degrees) and lack of normal summer rainfall, the garden plants are growing well in the waffles, while the weeds outside the gardens are dry and withered. The corn is planted in the old way, with four to eight kernels in a fairly deep hole. As the plants grow, the gardeners round the hills to support the stalks. They use a technique called intercropping, in which pumpkins, beans, and corn are planted in the same waffle squares. The pumpkin and melon vines spread out their wide leaves to shade the ground, which slows evaporation, keeps the roots of the other plants a bit cooler, and deprives weeds of light. Beans add nitrogen to the soil and help to feed the corn without using commercial fertilizers.

Zuni gardeners who use traditional methods say that besides seeds, only three ingredients are needed for a successful organic garden: soil, water, and manure. In a private waffle garden, one man uses well-composted sheep manure, some of which has been composting for over a hundred years. Because manure contains seeds, they often have to do a considerable amount of weeding, but they consider the result worth the extra work. This garden consists of two waffles inside a fenced area approximately sixteen feet wide and thirty-two feet long. The edges are mounded up approximately one foot around each space. In this relatively small space grow several types of corn, melons, pumpkins, chili, cilantro, zucchini, romaine lettuce, cabbage, and broccoli. Once a week, he trucks in water in two-hundred-gallon drums from a local lake. Including driving to and from the lake, watering the garden takes one full day. But a keen gardener does not mind garden work, and this man is no exception. Not only does he feed his family out of this garden, he enjoys the immense satisfaction that comes from being self-sufficient.

ZSAGP gardeners recommend certain traditional methods for entirely modern reasons. For example, they use a digging stick to avoid disturbing the soil any more than is necessary not only because Earth is the mother of the people, but because in this desert environment less disturbance conserves moisture and prevents wind erosion. Their modern digging sticks are near replicas

BROTHER CROW, SISTER CORN

of those used in old times. The only difference is that the blade may be marked along its length at two-, four-, and six-inch intervals, so the gardener can measure the depth of the holes. As always, pests are still a problem. Gardeners in Zuni must contend with Russian knapweed and bindweed, which they can control by planting rye. Caterpillars are a nuisance in cabbage if no one picks them off and kills them.

Families may sometimes cooperate in making a large garden, perhaps two or three acres. In such a garden, people grow traditional Zuni folk varieties of corn widely separated from each other to prevent them from hybridizing by cross-pollination. It is important for the Zunis to keep ancient varieties of corn pure, for certain colors of corn have sacred or special cultural significance. The garden project maintains a seed bank to ensure a perpetual supply of pure folk varieties—not only of corn, but of other crops, including Indian tobacco. These seeds are kept frozen in carefully labeled plastic bags so they will not be mixed up. The Zunis do not share these seeds of their folk varieties with outsiders for two reasons. First, some varieties have religious value, and cannot be shared without offending the kachinas, who might withhold their blessings. Second, these age-old varieties are part of Zuni intellectual property, which must be safeguarded to provide benefits to the Zuni people.

Safeguarding native folk varieties is important as well to a variety of organizations dedicated to preserving and promoting a range of native and heirloom plants. (Native plants are defined as plants that were growing wild in a particular locale prior to the advent of Europeans. Heirloom plants are those grown in the gardens of previous generations, usually of Europeans, which may or may not be indigenous to the United States or Mesoamerica.) One of these organizations is Native Seeds/SEARCH, an organization that, according to its mission statement, "works to conserve the traditional crops, seeds, and farming methods that have sustained native peoples throughout the United States Southwest and northern Mexico.... Through research, training, and community education, Native Seeds/SEARCH works to protect biodiversity and celebrate cultural diversity. Both are essential in our efforts to restore the earth." In total, their seed bank contains more than twelve hundred collections, many of which are endangered or rare. These collections are an important resource, as they include plants that have been adapted over the centuries to the most difficult growing conditions and that are resistant to or tolerant of pests, disease, and drought. These indigenous crop varieties are critical to maintaining the cultural identity of native people, and are also critical to ensuring a sustainable agriculture for the future—for all Americans. Founded in 1983 because of a request of Tohono O'odham farmers who wished to grow traditional crops but could not locate seeds, the group now works with many tribes in the Southwest, and with the Traditional Native American Farmers' Association (TNAFA). TNAFA, based in Arizona, is nationwide and includes representatives from nine tribes.

In the early morning sunlight, the plaza at Santo Domingo Pueblo is empty. At either end stand the kivas, round structures a full story high, with an outer stairway to the top, where ladders show against the sky. At the east end of the plaza, near one of the kivas, the shrine of Saint Dominic waits. It is a small, three-sided adobe structure, open toward the west. Long cottonwood branches or cut saplings lean against the shrine, their leafy tops mimicking shade. The cottonwood only grows where the water table is high, along streams; a thirsty tree, it symbolizes a plenitude of water in a desert environment. The one- and two-story adobe houses, including those along either side of the plaza, are also decorated with cottonwood branches, as well as a few corn plants. Inside,

BROTHER CROW, SISTER CORN

people hurry about their preparations. Dresses and shirts and trousers must be pressed, feathers placed correctly, mocassins brushed, and paint applied to bodies. For days, the women have been preparing food. Friends and relatives come from miles around, and tourists will inundate the pueblo. There must be water and food, especially for the drummers, the chorus, and the dancers, who will dance most of the day. It is hot this August, which is usually the rainy season. Everything is even more important than usual, for there has been no rain for a while.

Everywhere, people are praying their private prayers to God the Father, God the Son, God the Holy Spirit, and to Mary and to Saint Dominic, whose day this is. They pray, too, to the spirits, and all prayers are directed toward a single purpose—to cleanse the people so that they might do everything right and it will rain and the corn harvest will be abundant. In the Santo Domingo mission, the priests say Mass. At its conclusion, four men lift the statue of Saint Dominic reverently from his year-long resting place. Led by a man carrying a banner, and followed by the congregation and the priests, they carry him on their shoulders slowly through the pueblo. As the procession slowly makes its way to the plaza, the drums, low and throbbing like a heartbeat, sound farther and nearer, then farther again, until it enters the plaza at the west end and moves solemnly toward the shrine. As they walk, the people sing the Rosary.

The statue of St. Dominic is covered in gold, and from a distance shines in the morning sunshine. Some people who have been waiting in the shrine rise to greet the saint as he is set in place on a table at the back from where he will preside over the celebration. An elderly man says that he has come from his farm to attend the ceremony. He talks about rain, and how badly they need it for the crops. This is supposed to be the rainy season, he says. He explains that the two kivas are the two main divisions of the pueblo, the Turquoise kiva and the Ponca kiva, and that each is a different religious society. In first times, the spirits came to the people and danced, and called down the rain. But these are not times of faith. The real spirits do not come now. Men must dress up like them and dance the way they danced. When they do, though, the spirits come into their bodies, and they really are these spirits, so it's the same thing. His sons will dance from one of the kivas, but he doesn't say which one.

As the procession enters the shrine, the Turquoise kiva erupts in chanting and whooping. Men dance around the top of the kiva while the saint is being placed in his shrine, then dance down the stairway. Their bodies are painted from toe to head in grey, with black spots. Their hair is tucked under a sort of sock cut out for the faces, and on their heads is a topknot of corn husks standing straight up. Their black loincloths hang down long in front and back. Around their feet are ankle bracelets of shells, and each man carries a gourd rattle. Chanting and shaking the rattles, they leave the plaza and dance their way through the pueblo. They are calling the people to the ceremony, and people come to claim their chairs around the plaza and on the rooftops. All grows still. From the west end of the plaza, a black drum begins a rhythm as old as memory. The dancers, some two hundred men and women, move toward the shrine in time with the drum and the singing of the chorus. A man leading the dancers carries a tall pole as he dances. Attached to the pole is a long banner with a corn plant appliqued on it, and on top of the pole are balls made of red and green feathers. These dancers range in age from very young children to people in their mid forties. The men's torsos are painted white, their upper arms red, their forearms white, their thighs white, and their lower legs red. They carry a branch of spruce in their right hands and a rattle in their left. The women wear black, sleeveless dresses that leave the left shoulder bare. The skirts fall to just below their knees, and below the hem about two inches of white under-skirt shows. They carry sprigs of spruce in each hand. On their heads they wear the traditional *tablita* headdress, a flat wooden board about eighteen inches high and a foot wide by an inch thick. These headresses are painted turquoise and cut in the form of a cloud symbol with a cutout near the top.

They dance to the music of the drums and the singing of a chorus of around fifty men dressed in colorful shirts and trousers with silver conch belts. After approximately two hours the dancers change. Now the Ponca kiva enters the plaza from the west and dances, while the Turquoise kiva people line up to take offerings of bread and candles to the saint. The banner of the Ponca kiva has orange and yellow fluffy balls at the top, and its corn plant applique is darker. Unlike the corn plant on the Turquoise banner, the Ponca corn plant has no roots, but stands on clouds—red and yellow and blue half circles. Calling the rain, enlisting spiritual aid on the people's behalf. So it has always been, and continues yet.

SUGGESTED READING

A more comprehensive bibliographic listing is on file; readers may write to the publisher to obtain a copy.

Braund, Kathryn E. Holland. *Deerskins & Duffels: The Creek Indian Trade with Anglo-America, 1685–1815*. Lincoln, NE: University of Nebraska Press, 1993.

Buskirk, Winfred. *The Western Apache: Living with the Land Before 1950*. Norman, OK: University of Oklahoma Press, 1949.

Clark, Ella E. *Indian Legends of the Pacific Northwest*. Berkeley, CA: University of California Press, 1953.

Curtis, Natalie. *The Indians' Book. An Offering by the American Indians of Indian Lore, Musical and Narrative, to Form a Record of the Songs and Legends of Their Race.* New York: Dover Publishers, Inc., 1968.

Ford, Richard I. *An Ethnobiology Source Book*. New York: Garland Publishers, Inc., 1985.

Grinnell, George Bird. *Pawnee Hero Stories & Folk Tales*. Lincoln, NE: University of Nebraska Press, 1961.

Hunn, Eugene S. *Nch'i-Wana "The Big River": Mid-Columbia Indians and Their Land*. Seattle: University of Washington Press, 1990.

Hurt, R. Douglas. *Indian Agriculture in America; Prehistory to the Present*. Lawrence, KS: University Press of Kansas, 1988.

Keesing, Felix M. *The Menomini Indians of Wisconsin: A Study of Three Centuries of Cultural Contact and Change*. Madison, WI: University of Wisconsin Press, 1987.

Nabhan, Gary Paul. *Enduring Seeds: Native American Agriculture and Wild Plant Conservation*. New York: Farrar, Straus, Giroux, 1991.

Shultz, James Willard. *My Life as an Indian*. New York: Beaufort Books, 1983.

Trenholm, Virginia Cole. *The Arapahoes, Our People*. Norman, OK: University of Oklahoma Press, 1986.

Wilson, Gilbert L. *Buffalo Bird Woman's Garden: Agriculture of the Hidatsa Indians*. Reprint edition. St. Paul: Minnesota Historical Society Press, 1987.

INDEX